Piercing *the* Great Wall *of* Corporate China

Previous Books by Alan Refkin

The Wild Wild East: Lessons for Success in Business in Contemporary Capitalist China
Alan Refkin and Daniel Borgia, PhD

Doing the China Tango: How to Dance around Common Pitfalls in Chinese Business Relationships
Alan Refkin and Scott Cray

Conducting Business in the Land of the Dragon: What Every Businessperson Needs to Know about China
Alan Refkin and Scott Cray

Piercing *the* Great Wall *of* Corporate China

How to Perform Forensic Due Diligence
on Chinese Companies

Alan Refkin and David Dodge

PIERCING THE GREAT WALL OF CORPORATE CHINA
HOWTOPERFORMFORENSICDUEDILIGENCEONCHINESECOMPANIES

iUniverse books may be ordered through booksellers or by contacting:

iUniverse
1663 Liberty Drive
Bloomington, IN 47403
www.iuniverse.com
1-800-Authors (1-800-288-4677)

ISBN: 978-1-4917-9460-9 (sc)
ISBN: 978-1-4917-9462-3 (hc)
ISBN: 978-1-4917-9461-6 (e)

Library of Congress Control Number: 2016908778

Print information available on the last page.

iUniverse rev. date: 06/02/2016

Praise for *Piercing the Great Wall of Corporate China*

As managing director of a US accounting firm with a specialty in auditing Pacific Rim companies, I can personally attest to the underlying premise and motivating impetus for this book. China is too important a market and too big an opportunity to ignore.

Negative broad-brush publicity has blackened *all* Chinese companies, leaving US investors and joint partners with only two choices: completely abandon China or up their due diligence efforts.

Chinese companies exist in a unique financial, governmental, and business environment. As such, if you are going to participate in the Chinese market, it is essential that you understand and execute a unique due diligence methodology.

This is a book that needed to be written. It provides the tools necessary to perform forensic due diligence and evaluate opportunities.
Think of it as a Chinese toolbox made in the USA.
—Corey Fischer, managing partner, Weinberg & Company, Certified Public Accountants

This will be the bible on how to conduct due diligence in China. The authors have done a masterful job of walking deal makers and their advisers through the intricacies of Chinese society, which is indispensable in order to understand the cultural differences that make getting a deal done in China like no other place on earth.
—Lance Jon Kimmel, SEC Law Firm

If you want to peel back the layer upon layer of secrecy that surrounds a Chinese company and find out what you're really getting into, buy this book. There's no better guide on how to perform forensic due diligence on a Chinese company. The authors take their considerable experience in performing forensic due diligence in China and place it in an easy-to-comprehend guide for analyzing a Chinese company. This book will become the new standard for performing forensic due diligence in China.
—Scott Cray, coauthor of *Doing the China Tango* and *Conducting Business in the Land of the Dragon*

I have known Alan Refkin for twenty-plus years and coauthor David Dodge for fifteen-plus years. I have worked with both men on China projects, one as early as 2005. I worked with Alan helping small companies develop revenue streams, and I mentored David for many years in a small-company CFO position. Both authors are talented, experienced, and well educated. David Dodge is one of the most knowledgeable SEC/SOX people in the industry.

Alan Refkin is one of the most experienced people about China in the investment community. I have read and/or reviewed all of his China subject-matter books. This one is by far the most detailed and complete prescription for doing business in China or working with Chinese companies who want to be listed on US stock exchanges.

This book can serve two purposes: first, as a reference book for anyone thinking about investing in China, and second, for developing business relationships leading to an IPO with a Chinese company. It is a complete road map for either objective. All one needs to do is review the chapter headings and the subject matter within for a very complete education about dealing with the Chinese, particularly Chinese banks.
—J. J. Keil, cofounder, Keil Partners, LLC

Praise for *Conducting Business in the Land of the Dragon*

Drawing upon their years of experience "in country," Alan Refkin and Scott Cray have crafted a practical guide on how to succeed as a Western company in the promising yet pitfall-ridden Chinese market. Comprehensively referenced and meticulously constructed, it also addresses critical yet arcane issues, including intellectual property and cybersecurity, with the same ease and common sense that the authors bring to more traditional topics. The result is more than a primer. It's a plan for successful engagement for Western companies wishing to better understand and master business development in China.
—Rob Durst, CEO, Silver Bay Technologies

Working in the Latin American market, I've constantly been around foreign investors who fail to understand the challenges they must work through and the connections they have to establish in order to be successful in an unfamiliar country or market. When I went with Alan Refkin to China a few years back, I couldn't help but be utterly impressed by the way he made overcoming the aforementioned challenges look easy, despite the culture and language barriers. The speed at which he formed solid relationships with Chinese business owners, officials, lawyers, and accounting firms amazed me.

If you have to buy one book that teaches you how to conduct business in China, make this that book. You'll never find a better guide to take you through the reality of conducting business in China. Period.
—Jose F. Sada, president, DS Capital Partners

Having done business in China but now focusing on emerging Eastern European markets, I found much of the information contained in *Conducting Business in the Land of the Dragon* to be not only highly informative for someone conducting business in China but also applicable to other emerging markets. This is a well-written book for anyone who wants to go under the covers and see how business is really conducted.
—Tom Suppanz, director, investment banking, NESEC

Doing the Chinese Tango is a keen twenty-first-century guide to China and makes excellent reading for both experienced Sinophiles and China novices, offering insights into a wide range of issues. Everyone will learn from Alan's fascinating experiences and understanding of China, its people, its culture, and its future.
—John Lucas, director, Weinberg & Company, Certified Public Accountants

Praise for *Doing the China Tango*

I've been investing in, writing about, studying, and observing the world of small stocks and their associated successes, foibles, and failures for nearly twenty-five years.

I've been witness to a $3,800 investment becoming $4.2 million over a twelve-year time frame, and the demise of one of the great behemoths of all time—the pride of Rochester, New York. I'm referring to Kodak, the master of all things celluloid, whose complete failure to embrace the digital-imaging revolution led to its total undoing.

So, as a serial small-cap investor, I thought I'd found nirvana when I began studying the financial performance of the small stocks of China, which had navigated their way to US investors by listing on our stock exchanges and accessing our capital-rich markets. The valuations, profits, and growth rates had me swooning like a teenage girl in the front row of a Justin Bieber concert. With a little homework, patience, and luck, I was on my way to early retirement, riding the wave of the largest emerging consumer class in the history of the world.

As I was trained to do in my early days, I dug into the SEC filings, blindly believing the great accounting institutions of the twenty-first century had my back.

Alas, a substantial loss of my personal capital, along with a significant beating to my ego, was the result of not realizing early on that there is an entirely different and unfamiliar set of rules for doing business in China.

Without the proper guidance, you will find yourself stripped bare of your money and your pride in short order.

Had I met Alan Refkin earlier in the process, I might have been better prepared to swim in China's great-white-infested waters.

After working with and learning from Alan, I came to recognize that it's possible to do business in China, but only with the intrepid guidance of a grizzled veteran of the China business world.

Standards of integrity will evolve in China to a higher level over time. However, at present, China cannot be ignored; 1.3 billion people make for a very large global footprint. Very few of those citizens have much in the way of Western-style possessions, and the new generation of Chinese all want the same stuff we have. That's a lot of opportunity.

Consider *Doing the China Tango* your personal survival guide for doing business in China. Don't read it. Study it, and use what you have learned.

Had the aggressive investment bankers of the last ten years studied *Doing the China Tango*, a great deal of emotional and financial pain might easily have been avoided.
—Larry Isen, editor and publisher, EmergingChinaStocks.com

Doing the China Tango quickly and succinctly explains what China's business culture is all about. It should be required reading for anyone who is doing, or plans to do, business in China.
—Philip Abbenhaus, director, Asian Equity Research Institute

I knew Alan in his early beginnings in China's business environment. I believe *Doing the China Tango* reflects the disappointment—and the success—that a foreign investor faces in doing business in China.

This book targets the reality of conducting business in China and takes into account the country's culture, social outlook, mind-set, legal environment, accounting methods, negotiation efforts, follow-up, and finally … success. In my opinion, it's an excellent guide for anyone who wants to be aware of what's needed to be successful in working with the business and government in China.

—Jose F. Sada, president, DS Capital Partners

Alan Refkin: I would like to dedicate this book to my beautiful wife, Kerry, my best friend and partner in life. A kinder soul never existed.

David Dodge: I would like to dedicate this book to Shannon, for her patience and support of all my endeavors, and to Emma and August, for providing the inspiration.

Contents

Preface

We've been performing forensic due diligence in China for over a decade. During this time, we've learned that China is a unique due diligence environment that's unlike any we've encountered in other parts of the world. Chinese businesses play by a different set of rules. Checklists and procedures used in performing due diligence on companies in other parts of the world simply aren't effective in China. Culturally, socially, and philosophically, Chinese businesses function differently from those in the West and in other Asian nations. As a result, in order to pierce the great wall of corporate China, a new set of forensic due diligence procedures and methodologies is needed.

We use the term *forensic due diligence* for a reason. Forensic due diligence is due diligence that goes deeper under the covers. It essentially believes that you're guilty until proven innocent and that any numbers and facts presented during the due diligence process have to be corroborated and verified to a higher standard before being accepted. Standard due diligence uses a one-size-fits-all rule book that varies little from country to country. This approach doesn't always work when evaluating Chinese companies. Serious deficiencies within these companies are often overlooked, and business decisions are based on inaccurate information. This has resulted in a belief that no due diligence process could ever uncover all the deficiencies and fraud within a Chinese company. We want to change that perception.

We've incorporated our established procedures and methodologies into *Piercing the Great Wall of Corporate China*. In doing this, we've taken into account the realities of how Chinese companies function and operate, as well as how they interact with the Chinese government. We've experienced firsthand the great wall of secrecy that Chinese companies try to place around themselves. This has been largely effective at keeping those less experienced in forensic due diligence from discovering these companies' innermost workings. Few organizations and individuals, in our opinion, currently have an effective process that allows them to accurately conduct comprehensive due diligence on a Chinese company. The few that do keep their discovery and evaluation process proprietary to their organization.

In *Piercing the Great Wall of Corporate China*, we'll provide those who want to conduct forensic due diligence on Chinese companies with the benefit of our experience as partners in one of the largest and most recognized forensic due diligence organizations in China. We'll provide you with the evaluation tools and associated information needed to successfully analyze a Chinese company from a whole new perspective, enabling you to finally pierce the great wall of corporate China.

Alan Refkin and David Dodge

Acknowledgments

We're both thankful to have worked with the dedicated and professional group of individuals at Thornhill Capital for so many years. Whenever we required verification of data, translation of documents, or a myriad of other tasks that went into the writing of this book, they were there to help and assist us. They freely gave of their time, and for that, these authors are very grateful.

Zhang Jingjie (Maria) has worked with us on previous books and again has demonstrated what an invaluable resource she is in translating Chinese documents, providing us with requested data, and verifying the mountain of facts we give to her daily. Thank you, Maria!

J. J. Keil, founder of Keil & Keil Associates, has been our friend and associate for many years. J. J. has served on the board of directors of a publically traded Chinese company and has been a fountain of information on corporate governance, as well as management and sales procedures. He's given us the benefit of his many decades of experience, and for that we thank him.

Dr. Kevin Hunter, our technical guru, is in a class by himself. In the seventeen years we've worked with Kevin, he's unselfishly given us his time and has always been there when we needed the incredibly complex analyzed and explained in a language non-techies can understand. We both want to thank him for his invaluable help and his friendship through the years. In these authors' opinion, there's no finer technology consultant on the planet. We also want to thank his partner, Rob Durst, who is an oracle on intellectual property strategies. Thank you, Rob.

Steve Zhu, Corey Fischer, John Lucas, Clay Parker, Matt Ogurick, Martin Schrier, Jim Bonaquist, John Thomas Cardillo, Dawn Millan, Jonathan Strouse, and Lance Jon Kimmel are good friends in the legal and accounting professions who have provided invaluable business, accounting, and legal advice to these authors throughout the years.

José Sada, thank you for your flawless input and investment banking advice on cross-border transactions. In the nearly fifteen years we've worked together, your guidance has always been spot-on and greatly appreciated.

Scott Cray, Dr. Glenn Orr, Aprille and Dr. Charles Pappas, Cindy and Dr. John Cancelliere, Doug Ballinger, Lou and Nancy Kincaid, Ed and Carol Scharlau, and Glyn Williamson—thanks for being our sounding board over the years.

We'd also like to thank Sarah Disbrow, editorial consultant manager at iUniverse, who has provided immeasurable help to these authors throughout the editorial and publishing process. Thank you, Sarah, for your help and perseverance in getting this book published.

Lastly, and most appropriately, we need to thank our wives. Writing a book takes a great deal of time, and both wives have been supportive and generous. It wasn't always easy for them, but they took our daily household responsibilities off our shoulders and gave us the time necessary to complete this book. Without their help, love, and support—allowing us to close our office doors for the hundreds of hours required to place our thoughts on paper—we'd both likely still be working on the book's preface. We have extraordinary wives.

Introduction

In 2009, a rash of fraudulent business practices by Chinese companies began to surface. Almost every day, one could open a newspaper and find new allegations of financial irregularities or the absence of significant corporate assets that had previously appeared in the audited financials of a US-listed Chinese company. Soon no one believed that any public or private Chinese company was honest or that its financials could be trusted. Over the course of the next two years, fifty China-based companies were delisted from US securities exchanges.[1] The value of Chinese stocks plummeted, investors lost billions of dollars, and foreign financing for Chinese companies soon dried up.

Performing forensic due diligence on Chinese companies for as long as we have, we both knew that what the newspapers were now reporting had, in fact, been going on for a substantial period of time. We'd performed forensic due diligence on scores of Chinese companies and managed to uncover these same types of issues over the years on a multitude of the companies we examined.

A question we're frequently asked is "If Chinese companies have all these problems with the transparency of their financials and other books and records, and they commit outright fraud by claiming assets they never owned, shouldn't investors just bypass companies in China and invest their funds in businesses within countries they do trust?" The answer to that question is that not all Chinese companies have inaccurate financials, and they don't all commit fraud. The image of Chinese companies has largely been painted by the press with a wide brush that seems to envelop all Chinese companies, many of which have accurate financials and don't commit fraud. The task of those who want to conduct business with a Chinese company is to distinguish between the two.

As to the question of why someone should become involved in China, Jack Welch, former chairman and CEO of General Electric, summed that up best when he stated,

> If GE's strategy of investment in China is wrong, it represents a loss of a billion dollars, perhaps a couple of billion dollars. If it is right, it is the future of this company for the next century.[2]

China, as the world's manufacturing hub, as a land of 1.3 billion consumers, and as a country that's shown double-digit growth for three decades, is simply too important to the economic future of most companies to ignore. Many companies and individual investors choose to participate in this growth by acquiring, investing in, or forming a partnership with a Chinese company. Forensic due diligence assumes a critically important role in providing the information on which they can base their decision.

As we mentioned in the preface, Chinese companies seem to operate on a different cultural, social, and philosophical plane than businesses in other countries. The primary reason for this is that China has historically been an isolationist country, cut off from interaction with the global business community for all but the last thirty-five years. During this time of isolation, Chinese businesses have developed their own morality, ethics, cultural leanings, and practices. Western cultures, in contrast, developed their norms of business behavior—and an ethical and moral equilibrium in international dealings with one another—over a period of centuries. As a result, the methodology of forensic due diligence in China can vary widely from that performed in other countries.

What we provide in *Piercing the Great Wall of Corporate China* is the comprehensive knowledge base necessary to successfully perform forensic due diligence on Chinese companies. In addition, we've made an assumption that those taking advantage of our knowledge in this area would already have basic accounting and business skills. They would therefore supplement that existing knowledge base with our methodology and procedures.

If you want to perform due diligence in China, *Piercing the Great Wall of Corporate China* will provide you with the tools necessary to delve deeper into the business and financial fabric of a Chinese company and understand the obvious—and not so obvious—factors that make performing accurate and comprehensive forensic due diligence on a Chinese company so challenging.

Chapter 1

The Due Diligence Process

Due diligence is the research and analysis of a company or organization done in preparation for a business transaction.[3] This investigation is designed to confirm or dispute facts that have been presented by parties to the transaction, with the goal of preventing unnecessary harm should these facts prove to be in error and to uncover material facts that may not have been disclosed.

There are two primary categories of due diligence:

- standard due diligence
- forensic due diligence

Standard due diligence serves a broad range of interests. It employs a one-size-fits-all set of procedures to analyze all or a portion of a specific company or organization. *Forensic due diligence* is a much more comprehensive analytical process that requires corroborative verification prior to something being accepted as fact. According to Forensico, forensic due diligence uncovers red flags by going beyond the stated disclosures and conducting a substantive analytical process to uncover the accuracy of disclosures, the reliability of reported performance, the appropriateness of internal controls, and undisclosed risks.[4]

Within each due diligence category, the following are the most common types of due diligence performed:

- financial due diligence
- legal due diligence
- operational due diligence

Financial Due Diligence

> *Financial due diligence* is the process of understanding and validating financial information, both historical and projected. Financial due diligence may include reviewing historical accounting records and practices, verifying critical historical financial data, identifying potential accounting irregularities, and reviewing and stress-testing the company's financial model. This is the most frequently utilized category of due diligence.[5]

Financial due diligence is commonly separated into two primary categories:

- historical
- projected

Historical financial results reflect what's already been achieved and recorded. Financial statements are generated and compiled from transactional accounting records and documentation like sales invoices, purchase orders, inventory records, bank statements, and tax returns. These statements generally reflect how the company has performed during a specific period of time and the financial position of the company on a specified date.

Other supplementary financial statements, such as statements of cash flow or shareholder equity, are required for publicly traded companies. These may be prepared by management, or they may be reviewed or audited by an independent accounting firm. Analyzing the processes and principles used to prepare financial statements and the level of scrutiny that's been applied both internally and externally can provide critical guidance about the reliability and accuracy of such statements.

Financial due diligence should also involve a thorough analysis of a company's expected future operating results. This information is most frequently obtained from internally prepared corporate projections. Projections are most often in the form of a financial model that uses fundamental assumptions involving the factors that drive the company's business to produce a set of projected financial statements.

A financial projection is highly subjective by nature, as it typically involves making informed estimates about multiple factors, such as market demand, market share, expected sales volumes, pricing, cost of materials, labor costs, tax policies, availability and cost of capital, and innumerable other microeconomic and macroeconomic factors. Each of the underlying assumptions should be reviewed in detail and tested for reasonableness, and the model as a whole should be stress-tested using a wide range of assumptions.

When operating in China, both historical and forward-looking financial due diligence must be taken into consideration. This is because of the frequent use of deceptive accounting practices, which are commonly employed in China. These include manipulation of tax reporting, off-the-books cash transactions, false documentation, nonexistent customers, and other fraudulent financial practices.

Legal Due Diligence

Legal due diligence is the process by which legal professionals determine both the status and the consequences of an intended transaction. The status is comprised of the details of the transaction as well as their context. This helps expose hidden risks or liabilities, and it sets the stage for a determination of consequences. The consequences portion of legal due diligence determines how things will change as a result of the contemplated action.[6] In addition, attorneys will determine if there are any impediments that would prevent the closing of the contemplated transaction.

Legal cross-border due diligence, or due diligence that takes place in more than one country, takes into account not only Chinese legal requirements but also the legalities that pertain to another country. On occasion, these may not be in alignment, and conflicting legal requirements may arise.[7] For those conducting legal due diligence in China, we always advise retaining a Chinese law firm that is familiar with the legal intricacies of both business and finance law. They can help to obtain a resolution to many of the complex issues that accompany cross-border transactions.

Operational Due Diligence

Operational due diligence is the process by which due diligence is performed on the fundamental elements that drive a company's underlying business. Operational due diligence may include an examination of items like the company's business model, facilities, products, pricing, distribution network, supply chain, human resources, and competitive landscape, among others. The purpose of operational due diligence is to provide the party performing the diligence—such as an underwriter, investor, or acquirer—with comfort and independent verification that the information provided by the company, and being relied on by the party performing the diligence, is materially accurate and complete.

Due Diligence Procedures

Financial

Every company and every assignment is unique, with procedures tailored to each individual project based on the requirements of the party commissioning the due diligence—and regardless of whether the commissioning party is an underwriter, an acquiring company, an investor, a company's board of directors, or an altogether different entity. However, there are standard procedures that are commonly applied in the performance of forensic financial due diligence. Not every procedure is applicable to every company; in employing these procedures, you'll need to take into account the specific type of company involved, as well as the established goals of the forensic due diligence assignment.

Historical Financial Statement Review

The following procedures are standard for historical financial due diligence:

- Review the company's financial statements for the last three fiscal years (monthly or quarterly, if available) to include income statements, balance sheets, and statements of cash flow and shareholder equity.
- Analyze period-over-period fluctuations in key accounts on the financial statements.
- Analyze key metrics including, but not limited to, gross and net profit margins, operating expenses as a percentage of revenue, current ratio, debt ratio, return on assets, day sales outstanding, and inventory turnover. These should be compared period-over-period and relative to comparable companies.
- If applicable, speak with auditors about key accounting issues.

- Obtain reconciliations of all key accounts, if available. If the company's financial statements are audited, obtain these schedules, which are a standard part of the audit process.
- Review a list of the company's bank accounts and balances by period.
- Obtain bank statements and confirm bank balances directly at the bank. See chapter 11, "Independent Procedures," for an in-depth discussion of the bank confirmation process.
- Review accounts-receivable aging and analyze the age of receivables based on industry, geography, and other relevant factors.
- Review methodology to calculate bad-debt expense for reasonableness and proper application.
- Verify the existence and validity of sample key customers. See chapter 11, "Independent Procedures," for an in-depth discussion of the customer verification process.
- Review inventory listing and movement schedules.
- Perform a physical observation of the inventory, including test counts and comparing the results to inventory records.
- Review previous inventory-count procedures and results.
- Review procedures for calculating reserves for obsolete or slow-moving inventory, and proper application of those procedures.
- Review the makeup of "other receivables" for unusual items, as this is a common catch-all account for Chinese companies where material items may be hidden.
- Review other current asset accounts, such as prepaid expenses and deposits, as necessary.
- Review the company's list of property and equipment.
- Understand depreciation methodology and analyze property relative to governing accounting principles.
- Verify the existence and ownership of property, equipment, and land-use rights. See chapter 11, "Independent Procedures," for in-depth discussion of the fixed-asset verification process.
- Review other appropriate long-term asset accounts.

- Review a listing of accounts payable, noting concentrations, related parties, and other trends.
- Review taxes payable and verify that taxes are accrued in accordance with applicable taxation policies.
- Verify income and value-added tax (VAT) amounts with government filings. See chapter 11, "Independent Procedures," for an in-depth discussion of the tax verification process.
- Review other appropriate current liability accounts.
- Review debt agreements, noting items like collateral arrangements, acceleration clauses, conversion features, and contractual attributes that could trigger special derivative accounting treatment under US GAAP (generally accepted accounting principles), as well as other material elements.
- Review the makeup of other payables for unusual items, as this is a common catch-all account for Chinese companies where material items may be hidden.
- Inquire about and review off-balance-sheet contractual commitments, such as purchases or construction commitments.
- Inquire about and review contingent liabilities—including, but not limited to, pending litigation, underfunded pension plans, and potential product liability.
- Understand the shareholder's equity structure—including, but not limited to, issues like the effect of dilutive securities.
- Review a list of sales by customer and analyze for concentration of sales, period-over-period fluctuations, and other notable trends.
- Review a list of sales by product and analyze for notable trends.
- Methodically review cost of goods sold, including the allocation of labor and overhead, and the use of LIFO (last in, first out), FIFO (first in, first out), or other methodologies.
- Review profit margins by product and compare period-over-period trends with available industry information.

- Examine the components of SG&A (selling, general, and administrative) expense detail for each period, comparing period-over-period, relative to comparable companies.
- Examine the components of interest expense and verify that the interest expense is commensurate with the debt load and the terms of debt agreements.
- Examine any extraordinary or nonrecurring expenses.

Financial Projections Review

The following procedures are standard for projected financial due diligence:

- Evaluate the assumptions the company used to compile its financial model, comparing this to industry standards, the company's historical performance, and other relevant metrics.
- Evaluate the company's capital requirements based on its expected financial results.
- Conduct a stress-test model using a reasonable range of values for critical inputs.

Operational

The following lists provide documentation that should be requested from a company when conducting standard operational due diligence, as well as procedures that must be performed. As with the financial due diligence lists, these should not be considered all-encompassing or applicable to every situation. Each company, industry, and geographical area has its own distinctive characteristics that should be considered when preparing a due diligence information request list and a customized set of procedures.[8]

General

- Obtain an organizational chart and staff structure by department.
- Obtain the articles of incorporation, bylaws, and other pertinent organizational formation documentation for the company.
- Obtain the articles of association.
- Determine whether the chairman or other executives of the company have previously been officers or directors of any other enterprise.
- Obtain a departmental listing of employees that provides their names, job titles, compensation, stock options, and length of service.
- Obtain a distribution channel and sales network chart.
- Obtain a list of the company's competitors that includes a description or estimate of their operation, size, location, revenue, and market share.
- Obtain sales information on the amount of business provided by a franchiser, agent, or direct seller.
- Obtain a list of who in the company is responsible for contact with the company's main clients.
- Obtain a description of the company's business process, along with important elements or components of that process.
- Determine the adequacy of corporate insurance coverage, to include product liability.
- Obtain information on the company's advertising strategy and the carrier or media designated to implement this strategy.
- Obtain contact information for the company's legal counsel, primary commercial banking provider(s), and auditing/ accounting services provider.
- Perform a SWOT (strengths, weaknesses, opportunities, and threats) analysis.

- Obtain business and/or operating licenses, industrial qualification certificates, and certificates of authority.
- Obtain capital verification reports, capital increase reports, and any related asset-appraisal documentation.
- Obtain the corporate organization code certificate.
- Obtain the company's tax registration certificate.

Contracts and Documents

- Obtain documentation for corporate ownership, securities, transport-vehicle licenses, patents, trademarks, trade secrets, copyrights, and other intellectual property (IP) and intangible assets, to include the date filed (if pending), the organizational body issuing the patent, and the date issued.
- Obtain income tax returns and payment documentation for the previous fiscal year and the most recent quarter.
- Obtain copies of the sales-tax return for the previous fiscal year, along with the sales-tax return and payment documentation for the current month.
- Obtain documentation for internal controls, to include policies and procedures for finance, inventory, purchasing, production, and sales.
- Obtain a list of regulatory agencies that have authority over the company's business operations, as well as a copy of the regulatory permits issued to the company and proof of corporate regulatory compliance.
- Obtain documentation for corporate insurance, to include product liability insurance as well as key-man insurance for key executives.
- Obtain copies of résumés for key management as well as the board of directors, as applicable.
- Obtain copies of employment contracts.

- Obtain documentation on collective-bargaining agreements, along with side letters.
- Obtain copies of non-compete and/or confidentiality agreements.
- Obtain copies of the company's personnel policies, consulting contracts, employee-benefit contracts, profit-sharing plans, health plans, contracts with unions, employee stock-option plans, option agreements, performance bonus plans, and other employee benefits.
- Obtain copies of workers' compensation policies.
- Obtain closing contracts related to the acquisition or deposition of an asset over the past three years.
- Obtain a list of company contracts documenting the customer, value of the contract, terms, and payment schedule.
- Obtain a copy of agreements and contracts with subcontractors and manufacturers of products purchased by, or outsourced from, the company.
- Obtain a copy of all agreements and contracts involving the lease of a building, land, or equipment.
- Obtain documentation on sale lease-backs.
- Review contracts with primary equipment suppliers for the company.
- Document the company's bidding procedures.
- Obtain a copy of management loan agreements, perquisites, or similar arrangements.
- Obtain copies of bank credit-line agreements, loan agreements, asset mortgage contracts, guarantee contracts that provide assurance to another, or similar agreements.
- Obtain document verification for property, plant, and equipment ownership.
- Obtain a copy of agreements with the company's top ten suppliers, as well as copies of existing purchase orders.

- Obtain a copy of joint venture contracts or agreements, partnership contracts or agreements, or other contracts or agreements involving a share of profits or expenses as applicable.
- Obtain a copy, as applicable, of contracts involving corporate mergers, acquisitions, disposition of corporate assets, or a division of the company—whether or not a transaction has been consummated.
- Obtain a copy of contracts or agreements with major customers over the past twelve months. Also obtain information on how long the relationship with the customer has existed and the time remaining on the current contract.
- Obtain a copy of marketing brochures and advertising materials utilized by the company during the course of business.

Legal

- Document legal disputes, litigation, or complaints that have occurred in the past or are presently occurring. Also, document those that are pending or threatened, whether involving the company, its officers or directors, or a third party.
- Gather documentation in the form of correspondence, reports, settlements, or agreements relating to litigation and complaints, as well as threatened or pending legal action by a third party.
- As applicable, gather documentation on regulatory filings or disclosures with a regulatory body—and provide all correspondence, reports, settlements, or agreements relating to a regulatory body.

Property, Plant, and Equipment

- Obtain a schedule of property and equipment showing the original cost, acquisition date, location, departmental use, depreciation method, accumulated depreciation, collateral, and any other relevant data.
- Document the location and description of the plant and property.
- Personally confirm the existence of buildings, machinery, and equipment, noting their physical condition; compare these findings to the company's list of fixed assets.
- Obtain a list of surplus or idle buildings and equipment.
- Obtain a copy of the title to the company's property.
- Obtain any reports from third parties regarding the assessed and appraised fair-market value of any the company's property or equipment.
- Note restrictions imposed by building and zoning codes.
- Assess utility availability, usage, and rates.
- Document property taxes and other fixed costs.
- Obtain documentation regarding any liens against the property.
- Analyze preventative and emergency maintenance costs.
- Obtain a description and detail of planned capital projects.
- Analyze the potential technological obsolescence of equipment.
- Document equipment and property maintenance that has been performed, and identify the need for repair or improvements.

Procurement/Purchasing

- Evaluate the efficiency and autonomy of the procurement function.
- Perform a value analysis on purchased materials.
- Evaluate savings that have been realized, or could be earned, from obtaining a cash discount.
- Review whether materials and supplies are standardized throughout the company.
- Understand the relationship between procurement and production in regard to long- and short-term planning.
- Evaluate procurement procedures from the time a requisition or purchase order is placed through receipt of the items and subsequent payment to the supplier.
- Determine what percentage of short lead times for product and vendor purchases—given operating personnel—leads to a placement of urgent orders.
- Determine variances from price standards for product purchases.

Production

- Obtain a list of the main products the company produces along with a chart of the production process.
- Obtain a production schedule and ascertain how the company has adhered to this schedule.
- Ascertain the number of days it takes for a customer's order to be processed through the plant.
- Analyze idle production time resulting from delays or work stoppage.
- Analyze what amount of waste and scrap is produced in the manufacturing process.
- Evaluate what materials have been rejected after an incoming inspection, and the quantity of materials rejected.
- Evaluate economic production-order quantities.
- Evaluate the company's production methods.
- Analyze delays in product delivery.
- Analyze the amount of returned goods and the reasons for such returns.

Labor

- Analyze labor efficiency, including absenteeism, accidents, grievances, and overtime.
- Analyze labor turnover.
- Perform time and motion studies.
- Analyze subcontracting controls.
- Assess the availability of required labor.
- Determine if there are equal-opportunity employment issues.

Inventory, Materials, and Distribution

- Perform a trend analysis on work in progress and finished goods.
- Obtain details on the company's distribution networks.
- Analyze the company's bills of material.
- Analyze required storage and inventory-warehousing requirements.
- Analyze inventory controls.
- Document inventory turnover (ratio of the average inventory to the cost of sales) by product line and line of business.
- Document which basis was used in your evaluation, such as FIFO and average costs.
- Document which inventory is fast-moving, slow-moving, excess, and obsolete.
- Document what amount of stock has been written off over the last two to three years.
- Document how often physical counts are made and the extent to which adjustments are required.
- Determine the accuracy and quality of perpetual inventory records.
- Determine the security of the inventory.
- Evaluate how management is kept informed of inventory turnover, discontinued lines, and asset percentage.
- Document seasonal inventory fluctuations.
- Determine the availability and potential price variance of critical raw materials.
- Determine if there are multiple sources for critical raw materials.
- Analyze lead times required for materials and required tooling.
- Determine the company's proximity to transportation facilities and material sources.
- Compare the relation of material costs to sales over a five-year period.
- Determine if the company's parts inventory for the plant's manufacturing equipment is satisfactory.

Suppliers

- Obtain a contact list of material suppliers.
- Document purchases from suppliers over a two- to three-year period.
- List the various agreements with suppliers and the terms of such agreements for items like rebates and discounts.
- Document the company's dependence on a particular supplier.

Quality Control

- Analyze the company's quality-control function to include data on the type and quantity of defective production items.
- Analyze the quantity of returned goods and the reasons for such returns.

Health and Safety

- Obtain a description of the company's safety and security measures.
- Document health and safety considerations associated with operation of the company's machinery and equipment.

Environment

- Determine the company's compliance with applicable environmental regulations.
- Determine to what extent by-products and recyclable materials are used by the company in its production process.
- Document which recycled materials, and other ancillary company materials are sold to third parties.

Customer Service

Document if customer orders were unsatisfied because of a lack of product in stock, and if the customer was provided with a substitute product or had the ordered item placed on back order.

Government and Taxation

- Determine the local, provincial, and national government institutions that have authority over the company.
- Determine if the company's industry is being provided with incentives by the national government.
- Determine if the company has obtained all required government approvals for producing the company's product.
- Document whether the company has paid its tax obligations in full and on time, or whether the company still owes local and national taxes.
- Determine whether the company has a staged repayment-of-taxes plan in place with the government.
- Determine whether the government has received a report of illegal or irregular activity at the company.
- Determine if the government has provided subsidies to the company and, if so, how long the company expects to continue to receive such subsidies.
- Determine if the government has awarded contracts to the company and, if so, which contracts.
- Determine if the government intends to award any contracts to the company in the future.
- Access whether the company's production-approval documents from the government are complete.
- Obtain copies of the company's annual reports filed with the State Administration for Industry and Commerce (SAIC).

- Obtain copies of all quarterly and annual corporate income-tax declarations filed with the State Administration for Taxation (SAT).
- Obtain copies of all quarterly and annual value-added tax declarations filed with the SAT.
- Obtain formal government documentation related to any tax exemptions, incentives, or holidays for which the company qualifies.

Chapter 2

Corporate Records and Documents

Corporate China tends to be bureaucratic and paper-driven. By that we mean that the government requires companies to obtain a great many permits, licenses, and certificates in order to maintain compliance with both local and national laws. This documentation is most frequently not in an electronic format but exists as paper documents that have been stamped with the appropriate government seal.

> Corporate records and documents are generally among the first items reviewed during due diligence. They provide fundamental information about the legal and capital structure of the company, as well as the company's legal authority to operate in a given field. Understanding what documents are required, where to find them, and what they represent is critical to performing due diligence in China.

Organizational Chart

The first corporate document that should be reviewed—in order to understand the management and operational structure of a company—is the organizational chart. If a company doesn't have a written or illustrated version of its organization, it will be necessary to assemble this information at the beginning of the due diligence process.

An organizational chart is typically prepared as a flowchart showing the parent-subsidiary relationship with the entirety of its legal entities as well as the individuals responsible for various corporate functions. Charts can illustrate anything from the structure of a simple legal entity, which operates in one location and produces a single product or service, to that of an extremely complicated corporate entity with a number of geographically distributed subsidiaries providing various products and services. The organizational chart is a useful planning tool in helping you procedurally organize your due diligence and allocate resources.

Business Plan

In addition to the organizational chart, the company's business plan is a useful tool to provide context around the company's operating history, fund-raising intentions, and expected path. Items that can be corroborated in the business plan include market data and assumptions underlying financial projections. These assumptions may include expected product pricing, gross-margin expectations, or production volume relative to capacity.

Historical financial information and management backgrounds can also usually be found in a business plan. Documentation verifying the appointment of management can be obtained from the local Administration of Industry and Commerce (AIC).

Articles of Association

A company's articles of association lay out the purpose of the company, how various functions within the organization are to be carried out, how directors are appointed, and how financial documents are to be handled. The articles of association can also identify the manner in which a company will issue shares of stock, pay dividends, audit financial records, and define voting rights. This is essentially a user's manual for the day-to-day tasks of a company.[9]

The articles of association can be obtained from, and verified with, the local office of the AIC.

Articles of Incorporation

The articles of incorporation, also known as the certificate of incorporation or the corporate charter, are the primary rules governing the management of a corporation. It's the certificate issued by a government registry that confirms and validates the existence of the company.

A company's articles of incorporation usually contain the following:[10]

- the name of the company
- the company registration number or document number
- the type of company
- the official date of incorporation

Like association documents, incorporation documents and business license can be verified at the local AIC.[11]

Documents Required for the Formation of a Company

As part of the forensic due diligence process, it's important to understand the requirements for forming a business in China. Understanding this process will enable one to better examine a company's corporate records and documents and identify missing or deficient ones.

The process for incorporation and registration within the People's Republic of China is both complex and time-consuming. It consists, according to the World Bank, of the following process:

1. Obtain a notice of preapproval of the company name.
2. Open a preliminary bank account, deposit funds into the account, and obtain the certificate of deposit.
3. Obtain a capital verification report from an auditing firm.
4. Apply for the registration certification of a Business License of Enterprise Legal Person with the State Administration for Industry and Commerce (SAIC), the organization code certificate issued by the Quality and Technology Supervision Bureau, and the registration for both state and local taxes with the appropriate tax bureau.
5. Obtain approval from the police department to make a corporate seal.
6. Pay the fee for the organization code certificate issued by the Quality and Technology Supervision Bureau.
7. Register with the local statistics bureau.
8. Open a formal bank account for the company and transfer the registered capital into the account.
9. Apply for the authorization to print or purchase financial invoices and receipts.
10. 1File for recruitment registration with the local career service center.
11. Register with the Social Welfare Insurance Center.

Preapproval of the Company Name

The first requirement is to select a company name. The preapproval authority for this name is the local AIC. An application and required documents can be downloaded from the AIC website and then submitted to the local AIC office. Name approvals for applications submitted in this manner will take approximately fifteen days. If the applicant goes directly to the AIC office, the name of the company will immediately be approved or rejected at that time.

The following are required to submit an application for a company name:[12]

- The application must be signed by all shareholders of the company.
- Business licenses or other registration certificates must also be filed with the application if the shareholders are companies or other eligible entities.
- A photocopy of the identity cards of the individual shareholders must also be filed with the application.

Capital Contributions

China requires that a minimum capital contribution of 30,000 yuan (approximately $4,900 USD) be made when a company is established. If this capital contribution is in the form of cash, then once the company name is approved, the company can open a bank account and deposit funds. The bank will issue the company a certificate of deposit for these funds.

Nonmonetary assets can also be contributed. The shareholder would transfer the title of the assets, and the company would obtain an appraisal to determine the amount of the capital contribution. Shareholders can contribute up to 70 percent of the registered capital of a limited liability company in nonmonetary assets. Any remaining capital contributions must be made within two years after the establishment of the company.[12]

Capital Verification Report

Following a capital contribution, a person would need to obtain, from an auditing firm, a capital verification report verifying the company's capital. Filing this report is a legal requirement when a company is initially established, when corporate capital is increased or decreased, when there's a change in shareholders, and when the company is part of a merger or acquisition.[13]

The approval process takes approximately fifteen days. Once approved, the company will receive a "notice on approval for establishment registration." A business license will be issued within ten days.

Once the capital verification report is obtained, a person at the company will then need to apply for the following:

- a registration certification that, translated into English, is called a *Business License of Enterprise Legal Person*. This is obtained from the SAIC
- an organization code certificate issued by the Quality and Technology Supervision Bureau
- proof of registration for both state and local taxes, obtained from the tax bureau

Registration Certification

To obtain a registration certification, a person will need to file the following documents along with the application:[12]

- notice of approval of the company name
- proof of a company office, such as a lease agreement
- capital verification certificate or appraisal report
- articles of association, executed by each shareholder
- representation authorization
- identity cards of the shareholders and identification documents for the shareholders
- appointment and identification documents for the directors, supervisors, and officers
- appointment and identification documents for the company's legal representative
- documents certifying transfer of property title, if the initial contribution is in the form of nonmonetary assets

General Corporate Seal

Once the company is registered, a notice to make the company seal will be issued and the general corporate seal carved. This seal has the same legal effect as a legally empowered person's signature at the company. Chinese law dictates that the general corporate seal will be round, not more than 4.5 centimeters in diameter, and have a penta-star at its core surrounded by the name of the company.[14] If a corporate seal is missing or stolen, the company must report this to the police, as they will have to authorize the production of a new seal. In addition, the company will have to announce the loss of the seal in the local newspaper for at least one day.

Organization Code Certificate

The next step in establishing a business is to obtain an organization code certificate. The National Organization Code (NOC) is a unique identifier that's issued to an entity organized in China. It identifies the company as being duly established under Chinese law.[15]

The NOC must be obtained within thirty days of obtaining a business license. This certificate is issued by the Quality and Technology Supervision Bureau upon presentation of a properly completed application, along with the company's business license and a copy of the identity card of the legal representative.

The following documents must be submitted to the National Administration for Organization Code Allocation for a company to apply for an NOC:

- a photocopy of both sides of the representative office's SAIC registration certificate.
- a photocopy of the representative office's China Insurance Regulatory Commission (CIRC) approval certificate.
- the representative office's official seal.

Tax Registration Form

Once an organization code certificate has been issued, a tax registration form must be filed within thirty days of receiving the registration application. It can be filed with either the state taxation bureau or the local taxation bureau.

To complete the tax registration process, the company founders will need to file their tax registration form along with their initial tax reporting forms and the following documents:[12]

- business license (original and one copy)
- organization code certificate (original and one copy)
- identification card of the legal representative (original and one copy)
- identification card of the taxation personnel (original and one copy)
- company seal and financial seal
- office lease agreement and rent receipts
- articles of association (original and one copy)
- bank-issued account-opening certificate (original and one copy)
- capital verification report.
- property ownership certificate (photocopy)
- land-use right certificate
- commitment letter certifying the authenticity of the documents submitted

Statistics Bureau Registration

Within thirty days of obtaining a business license, the person establishing the company will also have to file an application and register with the local statistics bureau.[12] They'll need a copy of the business license and of the organization code certificate to complete the process.

Formal Bank Account

At this time, the person establishing the company can open up a formal bank account and transfer registered capital into the account.

Financial Invoices and Receipts

At the same time a company opens a formal banking account, it can apply for authorization to print or purchase financial invoices and receipts. In China, an invoice, referred to as a *fapiao*, is the method by which the government monitors the tax paid on a transaction. These invoices are printed, distributed, and administered by the taxing authority. The taxation authority issues the company an invoice-purchasing book, which it then uses to acquire invoices.

There are two categories of fapiaos: general invoices and special value-added tax (VAT) invoices.[16] The general invoice is used as evidence of payment and can be issued by enterprises or businesses that are not subject to the requirements of VAT, such as those in retail and consumer goods.

The special VAT invoices are issued by general taxpayers to their customers when selling commodities or providing taxable services. The fapiao is used as a valid proof of an expenditure. The VAT and general invoices are published by the tax authority for antiforgery reasons. Taxpayers buy VAT and general invoices from the tax authority.

To obtain these financial invoices/receipts, a company must present the following:

- tax registration certificate
- identity card of taxation personnel
- application form
- model(s) of the company's invoice seal

Recruitment Registration

A new company, within thirty days of being established, must register with the local career service center, sponsored by the local government.[12] The company can download these registration forms electronically.

Social Welfare Insurance

The last step in the process of establishing a business is to register with the Social Welfare Insurance Center within thirty days of establishing the company. This is necessary so that the company can pay the employee's social insurance.

To register, a company must provide the following forms:[12]

- company seal
- business license
- organization code certificate

Once all documents have been verified, the company receives a notice that it can now open a social insurance account at the designated bank. Upon receiving notification from the bank that an account has been opened, the local social insurance office will issue the company a social insurance registration card.

Business and Operating Licenses

The company you're reviewing should have the proper business license for the operations it's performing. That sounds simple, but we've come across a number of situations where the business license is for a function different from what the company is currently performing. Many times this involves trying to lower corporate taxes—as the operation the company is licensed for, but not performing, may enjoy tax exemptions or other incentives. In addition, as the company expands and diversifies, additional licenses may be required.

Be sure to look at all the functions performed by the company to determine if the company has the proper license(s). Licenses have an expiration date and include the name of the individual to whom the license is granted. Ensure that the license is current and that the license is with someone at the company and not a third party with whom no formal business relationship has been established.[11]

Joint Ventures and Partnerships

Any joint venture or partnership agreements should be obtained from the company. The terms of the agreements—and any potential impact on a contemplated transaction—should be reviewed and understood in full.

Shareholder Agreements and Communications

Shareholder agreements can be obtained from the local office of the AIC. Communications with shareholders—such as letters from the CEO to shareholders or transcripts of shareholder conference calls—should be reviewed for any potential impact on a contemplated transaction.

Equity-Holder Agreements

Equity-holder agreements should be reviewed to determine if there are any material special rights to which the equity holders are entitled. Examples could include profit distribution rights, special voting rights, rights that activate on liquidation or sale, or any number of other similar provisions.

Options or Warrants

Equity option and warrant agreements are far less common for privately held Chinese companies than for their counterparts in the West, since domestic financing transactions for these types of entities tend to be either in the form of equity, adding to registered capital, or ordinary bank debt. For Chinese companies that have already gone public in the US, copies of option or warrant agreements can be found in public filings, usually in a Form 8-K filed at the time the option or warrant was issued. In addition, detailed option and warrant disclosures are required in the company's financial statements.

For companies listed in the US, it'll be necessary to review the accounting methodology used for valuing options and warrants, as these valuation methodologies under US GAAP (generally accepted accounting principles) can be rather complex. Review the basic assumptions and calculations for reasonableness and compliance with US GAAP.

Corporate Financing

Documentation supporting any corporate financing transactions—such as share purchase agreements, debt agreements, registration rights agreements, or collateral agreements—should be obtained from the company and reviewed in detail for material terms that may be applicable to the contemplated transaction. Equity transactions should be compared to supporting documentation filed with the government, such as capital verification reports.

Board of Directors Appointments

Documentation appointing the board of directors can be obtained from the local office of the Administration of Industry and Commerce.

Press Releases

Where applicable, review any public announcements made by the company. Determine if both the context of the public disclosure and the material statements made to the public can be independently corroborated.

Chapter 3
Operations

The operations of a company not only generate recurring income but also increase the value of the company's assets. The greater the business income and business margin, the greater the sustainability and viability of a business.[17]

Operational due diligence is the process of reviewing the core operations of a company, such as production facilities, the production process, the supply chain, and current distribution methods. In addition, one of the primary purposes of operational due diligence is to analyze the ability of the company's existing facilities, as well as any planned capital additions, to deliver production at the levels outlined in the business plan. Operational due diligence may also seek to identify any inefficiencies in the production and distribution process that may pose problems for the company.

Production Process

Operational due diligence generally starts with a review of the manufacturing or production process. The following are among the common procedures that should be performed:

- Determine if there are any local or national restrictions that would inhibit the production process, such as building codes or zoning laws.

- Evaluate the efficiency of the production process and determine if the layout of the equipment is conducive to the efficient production of the company's product.
- Determine if the company has adequate storage for inventory as well as adequate warehousing facilities.
- Evaluate critical lead times for materials.
- Evaluate the effectiveness of the quality control process.
- Determine production costs, such as materials, labor, and other related manufacturing expenses; compare these to industry standards.
- Determine whether there are environmental issues in the manufacturing process.
- Determine if there's manufacturing seasonality.
- Analyze cost overruns and underruns, including relative size and frequency.

Suppliers

When performing due diligence on a Chinese supplier, you will need to verify the following:

- Is the business properly authorized? In other words, does it have all required business licenses and certificates?
- Does the supplier actually manufacture or supply the item being sold, or is it a middleman utilizing a website to promote another firm's manufacturing or supply capabilities?
- What are the capabilities of the supplier? Does it have surplus manufacturing or supply capabilities to meet forecasted future company demands?
- Does the supplier have an adequate quality control system in place?
- Does the supplier have any international quality accreditations? If so, obtain a copy and verify these with the relevant authorization organization.
- Is the item or items provided by the supplier proprietary and protected by intellectual property laws? If so, does the company

have the required intellectual property rights to manufacture or distribute the item or items in question? Do these intellectual property rights belong to a foreign company, and is there a dispute as to the use of the intellectual property for the item or items being sold to the company?

Outsourced Production

Many Chinese companies utilize the products and services of another company in meeting their manufacturing needs. Verifying these outsourcing companies is an important part of performing forensic due diligence on a company's operations.

In examining a Chinese outsourcing manufacturer, there are certain steps that should be performed as well as questions that should be asked. These include the following:

- Physically visit the company and view the manufacturing process, verifying that the products being manufactured are what they're purported to be and that manufacturing capacity is as described.
- Ask, "Does the outsourcing company have an adequate quality control system in place?"
- Ask, "Does the outsourcing company have any international quality accreditations?" If so, obtain a copy and verify any accreditation with the authorization organization.
- Verify that the subcontractor is in contractual compliance with the company in regard to service levels, transaction volumes, and similar metrics specified in the contract.
- Compare the pricing on invoices from the subcontractor to the company with the price paid by other companies in the same industry.
- Analyze the outsourcing company for any pressures that might adversely affect its ability to provide the company with future outsourced parts or services on a timely basis. This would

include potential staff turnovers and current contract awards that might strain the outsourcing company's capabilities.

- Review industry reports on the outsourcing company for relevant industry comments.
- Confirm that the outsourcing company has all required business licenses and certificates necessary for the normal conduct of business.
- Ask, "Is the item or items provided by the outsourcing company proprietary and protected by intellectual property laws? If so, does the company have the required intellectual property rights to manufacture or distribute the item or items in question? Do these intellectual property rights belong to a foreign company, and is there any dispute as to the use of the intellectual property for the item or items being sold to the company?"

In a number of instances, we've discovered that the owner of the company has a close personal and business relationship, or *guanxi,* with a subcontractor. As a result, the contract price of the item or service being provided by the subcontractor was higher than that found on the open market. It wasn't uncommon for those who have guanxi to share that price differential among themselves.

Production Equipment

In examining a company's production equipment, it is necessary to do the following:

- Obtain the location and a description of the plant and property.
- Personally view the operation of the production equipment in the manufacturing of the company's goods. It's important that this observation takes place while the production equipment is actively producing goods and not sitting idle. We've seen instances where Chinese companies claim their machinery is temporarily—and conveniently—down for regularly scheduled maintenance when, in fact, it's either in total disrepair or business is so slow the production line is not in use. It's critical to

view the production process in action to ensure that it operates as described.

- Determine who owns the production equipment. If it's a person or entity outside the company, examine the contract between the parties for compliance. If the production equipment is leased, there may also be accounting implications under US GAAP (generally accepted accounting principles), such that the value of the contract must be capitalized on the company's books despite the fact that it's leased. This occurs if the value of the lease constitutes a substantial portion of the value of the assets.
- Determine lease terms or depreciation rates and policies.
- Ascertain the market value of the equipment.
- Ascertain the technological obsolescence of the equipment.
- Determine if the condition of the equipment is sufficient to fulfill future contracts and if existing preventative maintenance measures taken by the company are adequate to ensure current and future manufacturing needs.
- Ascertain plant or land availability for production-line expansion.

Sales and Distribution

Many Chinese companies sell and distribute their own products, but a significant number prefer to use the services of a distributor. The primary reason for this is that they don't like interacting with consumers and feel that dealing with the public places a significant strain on company resources. The forensic due diligence performed will therefore vary depending on whether or not the company acts as its own distributor.

Companies that have elected to retain their own sales and distribution program often set up their own wholesale and retail arms. For instance, in the apparel sector, companies may sell directly to the consumer in addition to distributing goods to outside wholesalers and retailers. Many companies also have online distribution channels on B2C (business-to-consumer) platforms. In performing forensic due diligence on the sales and distribution function of a company, it is necessary to do the following:

- Review the contract between the company and outside wholesalers and retailers, as appropriate.
- Analyze whether there are established terms and prices contained within the contract.
- Analyze the amount of exposure for a product or service liability.
- Review whether the company's product can be sold in China, as some products, such as medical devices, have an involved registration process.
- Ask whether the company is in compliance with local regulations with regard to carton markings, product labeling, and related issues.

If the company outsources its distribution program, performing forensic due diligence on the distribution landscape can be very complicated. For example, some outside distribution agreements rely on distributors, agents, wholesalers, and sub-distributors to move a company's products to retailers and finally to the consumer. In addition, a distributor can also be an agent for the company, in all or only in designated portions of China. Many of these distributors also carry an inventory risk, as they're often contractually obligated to carry a certain amount of the company's product in inventory. The company customarily pays commissions and supplies the product at a discount from its retail sales price when utilizing outside distribution channels.

In performing forensic due diligence on external corporate distributors, it will be necessary to do the following:

- Review the company's contracts with distributors, agents, wholesalers, sub-distributors, and retailers, as appropriate.
- Pay particular attention to the title of the product, which could have material legal and accounting implications. For example, if a distributor is taking physical delivery of the product from the company, does title pass when the product is shipped from the company to the distributor? Or is the distributor selling

the product on consignment, in which case it has no financial obligation to the company until the product is sold to a customer? The answer not only affects who has liability in the event of loss or damage to the product but also has material accounting implications regarding when the company can recognize revenue. If a company consigns inventory to a distributor, then in order to complete a Western audit, auditors will likely need access to the records of the third-party distributor. This can often prove to be problematic in China.

- Find out if the distributor has represented similar products in the past and its success with those products.
- Obtain customer referrals from the distributor and inquire about any problems those customers may have encountered.
- Ask if the distribution company is in compliance with local regulations with regard to carton markings, product labeling, and related issues.
- Ask if there are there any disputes or litigation with outsourcing companies.

Purchasing

We've found that the purchasing department in some companies can be complex. Therefore, we usually begin by obtaining an organizational chart of the purchasing department to determine assigned responsibilities. In performing this due diligence, we recommend the following steps:

- Identify raw materials or products that are required for the production process. Ascertain their availability and price trends, as well as the time necessary to obtain these materials or products in response to a substantially increased product demand.
- Identify a concentrated reliance on a single supplier or small group of suppliers.

Inventories

In performing due diligence on a company's inventory, one would do the following:

- Analyze inventory recorded at balance-sheet dates and ascertain the reasons for major variations.
- Evaluate the adequacy of inventory storage and warehousing facilities.
- Analyze which items in inventory are fast- or slow-moving, which items are obsolete inventory, and what financial reserves have been recorded on the books to account for obsolete or slow-moving items.
- Identify critical raw materials.
- Examine the company's reliance on imports for inventoried items.
- Obtain any agreements on the company's inventory held by others.
- Determine how intercompany profit on inventory is treated.
- Ascertain the frequency and adequacy of physical counts and the quality of perpetual inventory records. Determine whether differences were adjusted in the general ledger.
- Compare physical inventories to perpetual records and examine corporate procedures for resolving variances.
- Determine the method used by the company to cost its inventory. Most companies employ common costing methods like LIFO (last in, first out), FIFO (first in, first out), or weighted average cost. In our experience, cost accounting in China is less sophisticated than in the West. As a result, the methodology of applying materials cost—and allocating overhead and other manufacturing costs—should be evaluated in detail with respect to the accounting and auditing requirements to which the company is, or will be, subject.
- Ideally, an independent physical inventory count should be performed to verify the inventory value being carried on the company's books. In our experience, it's common for Chinese

companies to overstate inventory on internal financial accounts compared with the amounts that are finally reported after a Western audit. This occurs for a variety of reasons, including sloppy cost accounting, unwillingness to create reserves for unusable inventories, unfamiliarity with Western accounting policies where inventories are carried at the lower of cost or market value, or sometimes outright fraud in an attempt to overstate net assets. Depending on the scope of the forensic due diligence assignment, a full inventory may not be viable. The process is labor-intensive and, therefore, expensive; it also requires the full cooperation of the company, as production usually has to be stopped for a period of time. However, even a scaled-back sampling of the inventory can be very valuable for identifying problem areas, and this can be expanded if problems are identified.

- Evaluate the internal controls and procedures over the physical movement of inventories and the updating of account records.
- Conduct a competitive cost analysis between the company's goods and those of its major competitors.

Human Resources

An analysis of the human resources function within a company requires that the following be examined:

- the amount of staff turnover and the reasons for it
- workplace accidents and the adequacy of the company's safety programs
- corporate working conditions
- the adequacy of the company's training programs
- the productivity of the company's labor force
- the company's employee benefit programs and whether they are in compliance with local and national government policies

External Factors

The areas described below don't fall into a specific operational category; nevertheless, they're extremely important in evaluating a company's operations:

- pending labor issues
- pending or anticipated government regulations, local or national
- the adequacy and availability of power for existing and future operational needs
- leases or contracts that are nearing expiration
- local government restrictions imposed by building codes or other laws that might affect property, plant, or equipment
- title to the property
- insurance coverage
- liens or condemnation proceedings
- potential litigation, including intellectual property issues

Analyze if any key patents and trademarks are held by management, shareholders, or other individuals and what rights the company has to use these patents on an ongoing basis.

Marketing Plan

Performing due diligence on the company's marketing is often one of the more subjective areas of a forensic due diligence review. It differs from areas like financial due diligence in that the goal is often to gain an understanding of interacting market and industry dynamics rather than to verify a set of facts, as is the case with financial due diligence.

Due diligence on the marketing function of a company varies widely depending on industry, size, geography, corporate philosophy, and other factors. In contrast to financial due diligence where—regardless of the size or industry—companies have similar financial accounts that must be examined, due diligence on the marketing function requires that procedures be tailored to each situation and does not closely follow a fixed set of steps.

If the company has a written marketing plan, the basis and underlying assumptions that drive it should be scrutinized, similar to the way in which the assumptions underlying a financial projection would be analyzed.

Industry Data

Industry data like market size, pricing, and market share are almost always created and published exclusively by the Chinese government. This information is often skewed to meet the country's political, social, or financial objectives. It's much rarer in China than in the West to find objective third-party market or industry statistics. These statistics can be useful in providing a rough view of the industry landscape but should not be blindly relied upon in making investments or strategic decisions. The investigator should also gather qualitative industry information on the company's competitors.

Promotional Materials

Review promotional materials to ascertain whether promoted product specifications, quality, availability of items, delivery times, and other factors are consistent with physical observations of the products and facilities.

Chapter 4

Other Common Documentation

Aside from basic corporate documentation, certain contracts, agreements, and documentation are common to a wide variety of companies and should be considered part of a due diligence review.

In chapter 2, we discussed some of the basic corporate records and documents that should be reviewed as part of a forensic due diligence assignment. There are a number of other relevant contracts, agreements, and documents that are frequently found in Chinese companies of varying industries, geographical locations, and size. Many of these records and documents are similar to what one might go through in a forensic due diligence review of a Western company. But, as with most things Chinese, when these types of documents are reviewed in a Chinese company, they require special consideration because of the many vagaries associated with Chinese business practices and record-keeping.

Bank Loan Agreements

> For small-to-medium sized enterprises (SMEs) in China, bank loans are the most common form of financing.

If an enterprise has outstanding bank loans, copies of these loan agreements—along with any related collateral or security agreements—should be obtained and reviewed in detail.

Bank loan agreements can provide a significant amount of information that's useful for basic cash-flow modeling. This information includes the loan inception date, maturity date, repayment schedule, interest rate, collateral description, and renewal/extension terms. These terms should be verified and compared to copies of the loan agreements. Where possible, the loan agreements should be obtained directly from the lending bank.

There are certain aspects of bank loans that are unique to China and should be taken into consideration when reviewing loan agreements. For example, it's common for the debt structure of Chinese companies, especially SMEs, to be heavily weighted toward current debt, or debt that matures within one year. Yet these loans often will be renewed on a year-to-year basis under the same or similar terms in the absence of a material change in the company's business or the government's policy.

While they're a normal part of the Chinese capital system, these rolling loans can have a disproportionately negative impact on the perceived financial condition of a company. For example, a higher concentration of current debt will reduce the company's current ratio, which is the ratio of current assets to current liabilities that is a commonly used indicator of liquidity. This can lead to overstated concerns about the company's ability to satisfy its debts as they come due, when in fact a substantial portion of the current loans are current in name only and are essentially long-term loans.

On the other hand, even if a company has an established history of rolling its current loans over from year to year, the vagaries of the Chinese banking industry, and the Chinese government's control thereof, must be taken into consideration. The Chinese government can act unilaterally with respect to lending to particular industries, geographical areas, or businesses of a certain size. For example, an industry that was targeted for growth three years ago may be overheated today, and the government can immediately terminate lending to that sector to slow its growth. When analyzing bank loan agreements and the effect of loans on the financial condition and prospects of an entity, all of these factors should be taken into consideration.

Another China-specific bank loan characteristic that should be taken into consideration when performing forensic due diligence is the collateral underlying any bank loan. Most commonly, companies use hard assets like buildings, land-use rights, production equipment, vehicles, or other equipment as loan collateral. A forensic due diligence review should first examine the value assigned to the collateral. If a valuation report has been prepared, the appraised value assigned to each piece of property should be analyzed for reasonableness relative to the net book value—that is, the original cost less any depreciation or amortization recognized in the financial books as well as the estimated net realizable value (the price for which the asset could be sold) based on a physical inspection of the assets. The credentials of the appraiser should be considered as well.

We've seen instances where assets of little to no value have been assigned an unreasonably high worth for the purpose of obtaining a loan. Many times the bank is aware of the inflated valuation, but many times it's not. In either case, it's prudent for the investigating party to understand this situation.

Bank Acceptance Arrangements

Another form of bank lending common in China is what's commonly referred to there as a *bank acceptance arrangement.* These short-term notes payable are lines of credit extended by banks. The bank then issues the company a bank acceptance note that can be endorsed and assigned to vendors as payments for purchases.

Bank acceptance notes are generally payable within a few weeks or months and are guaranteed by the bank. Banks generally do not charge interest on bank acceptance notes but rather charge a transaction fee based on a small portion of the total note value. In addition, banks usually require the borrowing company to deposit a certain amount of cash at the bank as a guarantee until the bank acceptance note is paid. These instruments allow the company to borrow money to pay vendors for raw materials and then repay the borrowing upon receipt of customer payments from the sales of finished products.

Documentation regarding these types of arrangements should be reviewed in detail, noting salient terms like the length of the arrangement, borrowing limits, length of borrowing, fees, deposits required, and other relevant material conditions. The ongoing availability of such arrangements should also be analyzed, especially in situations where the company relies on these instruments to fund a substantial portion of its inventory purchases.

Leases

Lease arrangements can range from items as small as computers or vehicles to an entire production facility. Where a lease arrangement exists, a forensic due diligence review should include a thorough examination of the terms of each agreement. The following are among the questions that should be asked:

- What is the relationship between the lessor and the lessee? Are they related parties, such as family or business associates?
- Are the terms of the lease on par with market values? If not, was another consideration given as part of the overall transaction and not documented in the lease agreement? An example would be other business transactions given to one of the parties by the other.
- Is the lessor a government entity? If it's a private entity, what is its financial condition?
- What is the length of the lease and any renewal terms?

- Are there any "option to purchase" terms in the lease? If so, this could not only impact strategic planning but also have accounting ramifications if the corporate entity is being audited under US GAAP (generally accepted accounting principles) or IFRS (International Financial Reporting Standards).
- For land and facilities being leased, are there any restrictions as to the use of the premises?

Property, Plant, and Equipment

Where property, plant, and equipment are material to the financial position or operations of the company, certain documentation can help substantiate the value of, and title to, these assets. Aside from physical verification of the existence of key fixed assets, source documentation with respect to the acquisition of the assets should be examined. Examples include the following:

- production facilities—purchase contracts, payment documents, supplier invoices and receipts
- buildings—construction contracts, construction completion reports, payment documents, construction company invoices and receipts
- vehicles—payment documents, distributor invoices

Land-Use Rights

The local estate bureau can be used to verify land rights that a company has purchased. A company can either have a granted use of the land, meaning ownership, or an allocated right to use the land for a specified period of time and purpose. Since the value of each of these rights is quite different, checking the price of the land is important in determining if the value of the land provided by the company is reasonable.

Moreover, the land ownership certificate(s) at the local estate bureau will provide you with information as to any land-use restrictions on the property. In some rural areas, land rights are held by a village collective.

In this case, the head of the village collective has to be the signatory on any transfer of property.[11]

Supplier Agreements

Agreements with key suppliers should be reviewed in order to ascertain key terms like minimum purchase commitments, pricing, availability of materials, delivery times, and other relevant terms that could impact production or profitability. The financial condition and stability of the supplier(s) should also be taken into consideration.

Customer Agreements

Any customer agreement should be evaluated to determine material terms like contracted sales amounts, pricing, product mix, and other related items. The financial condition and stability of the customer(s) should also be taken into consideration.

Business Combination or Disposition

If the company has recently merged with or acquired other entities, documentation related to the transaction—such as the sale and purchase agreement—should be reviewed in detail. It's also advisable to verify that the acquisition and equity transfer were validly recorded with the Chinese government by reviewing the post-acquisition documentation of the acquired entity, such as capital verification reports and articles of association. If any mergers or acquisitions are in process, relevant documentation like letters of intent and any due diligence on the company being acquired should be reviewed.

Likewise, if the corporate entity has recently disposed of a subsidiary, a major asset, or group of assets, relevant agreements regarding the transaction should be reviewed. This includes verifying the appropriate recording with the government. Documentation regarding any joint ventures should also be thoroughly reviewed.

Patents and Trademarks

The Chinese intellectual property system is relatively new. It wasn't until 1980 that China sought membership in the World Intellectual Property Organization (WIPO) and, soon after, in 1983, initiated its first trademark law. This was followed in 1985 by the issuance of the country's first patent law and in 1990 with the establishment of copyright laws.[18] China's recent establishment of intellectual property laws therefore contrasts sharply with the United States, which enacted its first patent law in 1790, and with Europe, which had a patent law first instituted in Venice in 1474 and in Britain in 1623.[19]

The administration and enforcement of intellectual property rights in China is still evolving. From a forensic due diligence perspective, the role of intellectual property in a particular assignment varies widely from case to case. Because of the complexity of international patent laws, and in particular the vagaries of enforcing IP rights in China, a detailed analysis of intellectual property rights should be carried out by a seasoned IP law firm if such rights are germane to the company's business.

Insurance

All insurance policies should be reviewed to ascertain coverage levels and related risk exposure. Property insurance in common in China, but other less-tangible forms of insurance—such as business interruption, product liability, general liability, and errors and omissions—are rare compared with the Western business world. Essentially, this is because civil litigation in China is vastly different from that in the US.

> The ability of a citizen to sue and realize any material financial compensation for something like a slip and fall, or even damage caused by a faulty product, is virtually nonexistent in China. As a result, there's virtually no market for these types of insurance in China when compared to the West.

For companies that are already publicly listed in the US or are in the process of being listed, the existence and sufficiency of directors and officers (D&O) insurance should also be evaluated. For listed Chinese companies, these policies can be extremely expensive, and some underwriters refuse to write such policies at all.

Chapter 5
Outside Parties

In our experience, the management of a Chinese company is usually well versed in the intricacies of running a business in their particular industry and well aligned with appropriate government officials. In China, having the cooperation of government officials makes it possible, or at least easier, to operate one's business in a profitable manner.

However, almost across the board, we find that Chinese CEOs have only a basic understanding of Western business practices, if they have one at all. This is especially evident as it relates to the rules and regulations that govern foreign public companies.

When a Chinese company goes public on a foreign exchange, particularly in the US, the outside parties it chooses to assist in the process can make or break the transaction.

Companies that list in the US are subject to the laws that govern the securities industry, including the following:

- Securities Act of 1933
- Securities Exchange Act of 1934
- Trust Indenture Act of 1939
- Investment Company Act of 1940
- Investment Advisers Act of 1940
- Sarbanes–Oxley Act of 2002 (SOX)

- Dodd–Frank Wall Street Reform and Consumer Protection Act of 2010
- Jumpstart Our Business Startups Act of 2012

These laws dictate the actions a company must take in order to become and remain public in the US. There are requirements for almost every aspect of life as a public company, such as how investments may be solicited, how securities become registered for sale in the marketplace, what financial and other information must be published and when, and what types of internal controls must be in place.

In addition to US federal securities regulations, a public company falls under the purview of a number of regulatory bodies. For example, financial accounting and reporting principles must be applied according to prescribed regulatory requirements. For US public companies, all financial statements must be prepared in accordance with US GAAP (generally accepted accounting principles).

US GAAP involves the application of a hierarchy of accounting sources, the basis of which are the Statements of Financial Accounting Standards issued by the Financial Accounting Standards Board (FASB). This also includes interpretations and other implementation guidance issued by the FASB, the American Institute of Certified Public Accounting (AICPA), and the US Securities and Exchange Commission (SEC).

Furthermore, US public companies are subject to the oversight of the Public Company Accounting Oversight Board (PCAOB). The PCAOB is a nonprofit corporation established by Congress to oversee the audits of public companies in order to protect the interests of investors and further the public interest in the preparation of informative, accurate, and independent audit reports. The PCAOB also oversees the audits of broker-dealers, including compliance reports filed pursuant to federal securities laws to promote investor protection.[20] The PCAOB, among other things, performs reviews of public company audits to ensure compliance with GAAP and with generally accepted auditing standards (GAAS) issued by the AICPA.

Aside from accounting and regulatory matters, many foreign entities that list in the US do so through the establishment or purchase of a US holding company, which subjects the company to the laws of the state in which it's domiciled. This will often trigger periodic state reporting requirements, such as annual reports and franchise tax returns.

A foreign company can also list in the US as a foreign private issuer (FPI) if it meets certain requirements. These requirements specify that the company is not a foreign government, that at least 50 percent of its voting securities are held by US residents, and that one of the following is true:

- the majority of its officers or directors are US citizens or residents
- more than half of its assets are located in the US
- its business is carried out principally in the US

This listing does not require a US-based holding company.

If these requirements are met, listing as an FPI has certain advantages over a direct listing. These advantages include, but are not limited to, the following:[21]

- FPIs are not required to file quarterly financial reports.
- FPIs have flexibility in what accounting standards they use (including IFRS or local GAAP), whereas direct-listed companies must use US GAAP.
- FPIs can present financial statements in local currency and do not have to translate to US dollars, as is required for direct-listed companies.
- FPIs are exempt from certain proxy rules and certain aspects of SOX.
- FPIs have more time to file their annual report after their fiscal year-end.

The rules that a US public company must follow include US securities regulations, accounting and auditing rules, corporate governance standards, stock exchange requirements, and other regulatory requirements mandated by states and the national government. These rules are infinitely complex and constantly changing.

Even for a US businessperson, establishing funding and maintaining the regulatory requirements for a public company require the assistance of multiple professionals. For Chinese businesspeople, the situation is equally critical but inherently more complex, as they're far more familiar with Chinese regulations. They're only scantly familiar with US regulations, usually by hearsay or by educational presentations conducted within China.

However, even if Chinese businesspeople do have some knowledge of US regulatory requirements, they don't usually recognize the critical need for professional assistance. Instead, they normally ascribe to the attitude of addressing an issue only after it's been brought to their attention by a regulatory body or it's clear that a failure to comply will result in an inability to file a required form or other necessary document.

> For a Chinese CEO who has only a basic understanding of the legal and regulatory environment, choosing the right third-party advisers is critical. Without the proper support system, a transaction can be dead in the water from regulatory failure before it even has a chance to get started, regardless of the strength of the underlying business.

When performing forensic due diligence on a Chinese company, it's important to understand what third-party relationships are in place, who the third parties are, and what impact these relationships have on the company and the due diligence review. This is irrespective of whether there is a direct impact on operations, the compliance environment, the public's perception of the company, or another area altogether.

Investment Banking Firms and Third-Party Organizations

One of the principal reasons Chinese companies list in the US is to raise capital. In some cases, we've been retained to perform due diligence on behalf of an investment banking firm that's been engaged by, or is contemplating being engaged by, a Chinese company that wants to become listed in the US and raise foreign capital. In other instances, we may be engaged by the company itself, shareholders or debt-holders of the company, or other third parties. In all of these instances, the first course of action is to analyze the investment banking firm or other third party involved.

Key factors that should be considered when evaluating an investment banking firm or third-party organization include:

- the size, experience, and reputation of the firm
- the firm's experience investing in Chinese companies, including any notable successes or failures
- the quality of the team assigned to the engagement, including whether there are any native Chinese

In addition, we review and interpret the amount, type, and quality of any due diligence performed by the investment banking firm or third-party organization in connection with its representation of the company. Generally speaking, the type of due diligence performed by these firms shares some aspects with the forensic due diligence we perform. However, their approach is materially different.

These firms tend to conduct *business* due diligence, meaning that they mostly focus on items like the company's business model, strategies, products, pricing, production capacity, capital requirements, competitive landscape, and growth opportunities. In its simplest form, their due diligence involves an examination of how the business will be monetized and thus create a return on the investment bank's funding. This type of information can be very helpful in understanding what drives the company's business and identifying areas in which further forensic analysis should be carried out.

But investment bankers and most third-party organizations are not accountants, and their due diligence tends to be limited to the financial area. Their evaluation will often encompass a detailed review of the assumptions and inputs that drive the company's financial model, as well as an analysis of the historical financial results. But these analyses tend to be performed in the context of how they will affect future operating results, cash flow, stock price, and other performance metrics, rather than in an attempt to test the veracity of the underlying data. Forensic due diligence takes this approach further by attempting to authenticate the fundamental elements of the business.

> Due diligence performed by an investment-banking firm or third-party organization cannot be blindly relied upon. However, a reputable firm with an understanding of Chinese business practices can provide valuable guidance on areas that require a more detailed investigation.

Legal Advisers

> The quality of both domestic and foreign legal counsel involved in a cross-border transaction is very important and should be given due consideration.

Another important third-party consideration is the quality of a company's legal advisers and what type of due diligence they've performed. For a Chinese company going public in the US, having a strong US counsel is one of the most important aspects of the process. US counsel will advise the company on all manner of securities and other legal matters, and will often assist in the preparation of SEC filings—such as registration statements and Form 8-K material events disclosures. The Chinese company will also typically engage local People's Republic of China (PRC) counsel to assist with all matters related to PRC law.

With respect to both domestic and foreign counsel, and as with hiring an investment-banking firm, the experience and reputation of the law firm can be strong indicators of the quality of work being performed.

It's also critical that a US law firm have a presence in China with domestic Chinese staff trained in US law. This is usually accomplished either by establishing a satellite law office within China or through a relationship with a Chinese law firm. A presence in China is extremely important because it will be necessary for the law firm to speak directly with the company's management and staff on a timely basis to explain complex legal matters in the Chinese language. Non-Chinese members of a law firm, no matter how good their language training, never seem to be able to convey the subtleties that are necessary to adequately explain the law to someone whose only language is Chinese.

In our experience, it's unwise to blindly rely on advice, or even endorsed legal opinions, provided by local Chinese law firms. This is not because Chinese law firms don't understand or misinterpret Chinese law. On the contrary, they tend to have a keen understanding of the law and the methods their clients use to work the system in China. However, we've found that a great many local Chinese law firms have little respect for any governmental or regulatory authority outside of China. Their legal advice reflects this view.

Chinese businesspeople are suspicious and, as a practical matter, distrustful of those who are not Chinese. This distrust may extend to Chinese who are outside their company or specific geographical area. Chinese businesspeople often refer to themselves as insiders, while anyone outside their trusted group of friends and associates is an outsider. This inherent distrust of outsiders is very common in the Chinese business mind-set. It can result in advice being given to those who are not Chinese, or even to Chinese who are not directly involved in the transaction, that is misleading, incomplete, or outright incorrect in an effort to protect the interests of the client.

Of course, this outsider/insider mind-set isn't found in every Chinese law firm. Larger Chinese law firms tend to be more pragmatic and have the standards and ethics usually associated with Western law firms. In our experience, however, the outsider/insider mentality is very prevalent in smaller and local Chinese law firms.

In a forensic due diligence review, we recommend procedures to verify information or opinions provided by local counsel. As an example, PRC counsel is often asked to provide a formal opinion regarding the appropriateness of taxation matters, such as whether a tax exemption applies to the company, whether tax holidays were appropriately applied, or whether a waiver letter from the tax bureau is legally valid. This request is typically made by the company's independent auditors to supplement their audit work. We analyze the items opined on by counsel and evaluate them based on our experience in similar situations and our knowledge of applicable laws. If the information is contradictory to our understanding of the laws or of a complex legal nature, we recommend that the company engage a large national PRC firm with a strong reputation to review the opinion and confirm the facts therein.

Auditors

> The quality of audit work performed on Chinese companies can vary widely. As a matter of course, audit procedures are constantly evolving.

In our dealings with dozens of Chinese companies over the years, we've worked with a great many domestic and foreign audit firms. It's no exaggeration to say that we've found both the quality and thoroughness to vary widely. On one hand, we've seen Chinese companies audited by small US firms that don't have a single Chinese-speaking employee and subsequently subcontract their fieldwork to a Chinese audit firm. On the other hand, we've worked with companies audited by Big Four accounting firms where the entire engagement was planned and carried out by highly experienced Chinese-speaking auditors and management. In both situations, when we're engaged to perform a due diligence review, we look closely at the experience of the staff and for any published errors, glaring omissions, or misleading information in their historical financial statements. We also interview the company's financial management team, which works closely with the auditors, and ascertain how certain aspects of the audit were performed.

If possible, we prefer to also speak directly with the audit firm, though auditors tend to be very guarded in what they disclose of their audit methodology. In our experience, there's not necessarily a direct correlation between the size or reputation of the audit firm and the quality of work they produce in China. What really matters is local experience, the ability to customize procedures to local nuances, and the appropriate amount of professional skepticism.

This is one of the principal reasons we analyze the work performed by the audit firm. In our forensic analysis, we determine how the firm adapted its audit to fit the idiosyncrasies of the industry, local environment, and China in general. For example, if auditors performed a comprehensive in-person study, confirming customers and receivable balances—including researching the existence and validity of each customer—we might take their results into consideration in preparing the scope of our customer confirmation work. On the other hand, if the audit work indicated that some customers could not be contacted or that the company's receivable balances were growing older with no clear-cut explanation, even in cases where the auditors were able to meet their requirements and sign off on the audit without recognizing a dramatically large bad-debt reserve, these facts may lead us to focus more on our channel-check analysis.

The inquiries we make are specific to the circumstances of each company. However, there are common problem areas associated with Chinese audits that seem to come up again and again. These tend to be areas of which auditors are also aware and to which they pay more attention. However, we've found that the level of independent corroboration performed by auditors in these areas varies widely from audit to audit and firm to firm. As a result, we seek to understand the procedures performed and the rationale for doing it in that particular manner.

The following are examples of areas that could provide insight as to the quality of the audit work that's been performed:

- Were accounts receivable confirmations performed in person or by mail? What was the response rate?
- What type of work did the auditors perform with respect to the aging of accounts receivable and related bad-debt reserve?
- Were bank confirmations performed in person at the bank branch or by mail?
- What confirmation procedures were performed with respect to taxation, including VAT and income tax?
- If complex financing instruments were used, how were the accounting implications analyzed, including the calculation of fair value and an analysis of any derivatives?

The amount and quality of any work performed in these areas by the auditors gives us a good road map to the level of corroboration we need as we perform our forensic analysis.

In some cases, we've been engaged to provide an independent analysis of issues identified by the audit firm that prevented the firm from issuing an opinion—or, in some cases, even resulted in the auditors' resignation. In others, we've been called on to examine the methodology used by the company (and signed off on by the auditors) to estimate provisions for uncollectible accounts. Often during our examinations, we find that the procedures performed by the auditors in these types of critical areas were insufficient or that their conclusions were not well informed.

For example, we performed an assignment where the auditors had resigned because of what they believed to be audit inconsistencies, including a situation where they made site visits to a small number of customers to which receivable confirmations had been mailed and discovered that the addresses were located in residential areas. Upon examination, we determined that, for certain of these customers, the contact person responsible for completing the confirmation had provided a home address to expedite the confirmation process. This was due to the company contacting them and explaining the importance of sending a response so the US audit could be completed. To keep the confirmation from being delayed or lost in corporate mail—and not being familiar with the mailed confirmation process, which is not a common practice in China—the individuals instructed the company to have the confirmations mailed directly to their personal residences. The confirmations were immediately completed and returned, but the home addresses raised a red flag with the auditors.

We visited the individuals who completed the confirmations at their place of work, interviewed them, had them complete a new confirmation in our presence, confirmed that their home residence was the location to which the confirmation was mailed by viewing their government identification card, and confirmed that they actually held the position they claimed by viewing their business card and interviewing their coworkers. In this example, what an auditor thought was a red flag turned out to be a misunderstanding that was clarified by a more thorough analysis of the situation.

The quality of audit work varies widely across different types of firms. As with legal advisers, it's unwise to blindly assume that simply because Chinese financial statements are audited, they are correct. It's also incorrect to assume that the bigger the auditing firm, the better. As with most things, the experience and quality of the management and staff involved in the audit process are usually the determining factors in the accuracy of the audit produced.

In planning and performing a forensic due diligence review, the foundation laid by previous audit work can provide valuable guidance about where due diligence efforts should be more or less focused. The breadth and depth of audit procedures that were performed in critical areas—such as customer verification, cash verification, and taxation matters—can identify significant problem areas only where US-style audit procedures were applied and no consideration was given to Chinese nuances. Conversely, these audit procedures can highlight detailed China-specific procedures that provide evidence of company compliance that tends, in our experience, to be somewhere in the middle. Past audit work is certainly not a replacement for due diligence procedures, but it can provide hints that assist the due diligence professional to better tailor procedures and maximize efficiency.

Accounting Support

> For Chinese companies that list in the US, hiring the correct internal accounting professionals can be the most important decision they make.

Internal accounting professionals are individuals who are employed by the company and act as the company's agent in preparing financial information on its behalf. This is in contrast to auditors, whose job it is to test the accuracy of the financial statements that the company prepares.

When we're engaged to perform a forensic due diligence review, another critical area that we focus on is the makeup of the company's internal financial team. The professional depth and quality of this team can provide critical guidance as to where issues are more than likely to arise. This is an area where proactive correction of the team's makeup can be very valuable to the company in helping to achieve and maintain its public listing. In our experience, despite the understandable aversion of CEOs and investors to overspending on professionals, it's almost always beneficial to all parties to put the right accounting support in place from the beginning.

When a Chinese company is going public, it's generally required to complete either a two- or three-year historical audit, plus an audit of any interim periods since the end of the last fiscal year. This is a major undertaking that requires the supervision of someone experienced, not only in the fundamental process of aggregating an accurate set of books and records but also in the nuances of US GAAP and the US auditing process. Without the proper team in place, the initial listing process can be delayed by months and may even extend to subsequent quarters and even years. During this time the dynamics of the transaction may change, or funding may evaporate altogether.

Furthermore, once listed, all the hard work of becoming public can be erased with one late filing. Therefore, having the right people in place who understand the compliance environment is crucial. In our opinion, it's best to staff with the correct team from the beginning, even if the company and its investors consider the cost to be high. This is because any loss in market value stemming from compliance issues will usually outweigh, many times over, the investment made in hiring the right people.

The financial-compliance aspect of being a US public company is something that Chinese management has historically been poorly equipped to handle. The typical company in this situation is transformed, in a matter of months, from a private entrepreneurial enterprise with little to no reporting requirements outside of taxation to a completely transparent publicly held entity. The company must now report detailed financial and business information every quarter, in accordance with complex foreign accounting practices and subject to audit or review by a third-party auditor, all in a very limited time frame. Quarterly financial reports—which are subject to a review and not an audit—and procedures by an independent auditor are all due within forty to forty-five days after the end of each quarter, depending on the size of the company. Audited annual reports are due within sixty to ninety days after the end of each quarter, also depending on the size of the company.

We've found that companies going through the public listing process often encounter several common problems that, if not properly addressed, can lead to late filings, restatements, delisting, SEC inquiries, and other issues. Many of these problems can be avoided by engaging the proper accounting professionals, whose processes and methodologies most often ensure such problems don't occur. The more common pitfalls we've experienced in our work with scores of Chinese companies include the following:

- Chinese accounting and inventory systems tend to be highly manual compared to those of comparably sized US companies. This leads to a longer time requirement to close the company's books at the end of the period, and thereby results in more errors than encountered in automated systems.
- Local books are generally kept in accordance with Chinese GAAP and must therefore be converted to US GAAP for US-listed Chinese companies.
- Transactions completed by the company's entities outside of China—such as mergers with US or other offshore holding companies, or financing transactions completed in the US—often require very complicated accounting procedures that are often not understood by the Chinese company's financial management team.
- Thorough and accurate consolidations of multiple legal or operating entities, including eliminations of intercompany amounts and consolidation of equity accounts, are rarely performed by Chinese companies.
- Rarely do Chinese companies have senior financial employees who can speak English fluently or have a knowledge of technical

accounting terms that they can then accurately translate from Chinese to English.

- Chinese companies usually lack even a basic knowledge of the compliance requirements they'll encounter once they become public, including the following:
    - what forms must be filed with the SEC and in what time frame
    - how to prepare disclosures required in those filings
    - how to effectively work with independent auditors to make sure audits or reviews are completed in time for the filing to be made
    - how to prepare documents in the format required by the SEC
    - how to handle administrative and compliance matters regarding trading of the company's securities, such as removal of stock legends
    - how to comply with the internal-control reporting requirements of SOX

We frequently see these issues with Chinese companies going public in the US. Any one of these issues, by itself, could derail the entire listing process. When they are combined, it's typically just a matter of time before something goes wrong. According to a report by *ABC News* in January 2013, from 2011 to 2012 more than forty Chinese companies were delisted from the NASDAQ.[22]

To avoid these issues, we recommend that Chinese companies listing in the US employ several levels of third-party accounting support. As a first step, the company should engage an independent third party to provide audit support and compilation services. We recommend that the team be comprised of native Chinese accountants—preferably those who have worked in Chinese industry, as opposed to those who have worked in Chinese accounting firms. We emphasize native Chinese accountants because it's critical that these individuals be able to read and write Chinese as well as be familiar with the transaction-level mechanics of typical deceptive accounting practices. These individuals should work on a daily basis with the company's accounting staff to do the following:

- Fine-tune the accounting processes so that data can be consolidated quickly and easily.
- Assist with the process of consolidating all entities.
- Make conversions between Chinese and US GAAP.
- Perform accounting of offshore entities and any unusual complex transactions that require special accounting under US GAAP.
- Help the accounting staff prepare documents required for the independent auditor review or audit.
- Work with auditors to ensure that proper and thorough documentation is provided on a timely basis during the review or audit.

We also recommend that companies hire a CFO who has extensive experience working in the public realm. Ideally, this would be a Chinese-speaking CFO who was educated in and/or has worked for a public company in the West. However, in our opinion, there's a shortage of these individuals, thereby necessitating the hiring of a Western CFO with public-company experience.

If a company retains its pre-public Chinese CFO and utilizes that individual in the same position once it becomes public, this is usually regarded as a red flag. This is because the vast majority of Chinese CFOs simply don't have the experience or training to handle the responsibilities of a public-company CFO. There are many reasons for this, over and above a general lack of regulatory and financial knowledge. For example, the CFO must be able to communicate directly with the company's shareholders—who, in the case of a US listing, are predominantly US-based institutions and individuals.

In smaller public companies, the responsibility for preparing the company's SEC filings falls to the CFO. In larger companies, a separate accounting manager, controller, or similar position may be created.

Regardless, an individual with extensive experience in SEC filings should be hired to handle this critical task.

When a Chinese company lists in the US, it becomes subject to the requirements of SOX. Among these requirements is that public companies must include in their periodic financial filings an assessment of the effectiveness of their internal controls over financial reporting. For larger public companies, the testing underlying the assessment must be audited by an independent certified audit firm.

Generally speaking, internal controls in Chinese companies are poor relative to companies in the US, both in practice and in terms of documentation. In order to comply with SOX, management must carry out a fairly complex analysis of the effectiveness of internal controls pursuant to prescribed guidelines. In our experience, even newly public US companies have difficulty understanding and implementing the internal-control provisions of SOX. For a Chinese company, it's nearly impossible without outside assistance. We recommend that Chinese companies engage a SOX-implementation firm or expert to evaluate the internal-control environment, properly document policies and procedures, design and carry out a test plan, assist with remediation of weak controls, and prepare disclosures required in the company's public filings.

When planning a forensic due diligence assignment, the makeup of the company's accounting team should be given considerable weight. The due diligence provider must understand the expertise and limitations of the personnel providing information and decide if such information is reliable on its face or requires additional independent verification.

The mere presence of the outside parties discussed in this chapter should not be a substitute for the critical procedures that need to be performed in a comprehensive forensic due diligence assignment. The due diligence provider should consider the types of review and verification procedures that outside parties have already performed. The procedures performed, along with the related findings, can be valuable resources in pinpointing, among other things, where subsequent due diligence work should be focused, the level of verification required, and the number of items to be tested.

Chapter 6
Human Resources

Organizational Chart

Chinese organizational charts differ significantly from those in the West. In a Western company, employees often work in an open environment and are empowered to communicate among themselves to accomplish their objectives. They can answer questions, coordinate among various departments within the company, and find creative ways to solve problems and deliver results.

A Chinese company, on the other hand, tends to be a hierarchical organization that is governed by senior management directing the workers below. In this type of structure, only senior management makes decisions, and the management style tends to be dictatorial and directive-oriented.[23]

> This management philosophy can be traced back to the time of Confucius when, in Confucian philosophy, all relationships were deemed unequal and ethical behavior demanded that inequalities be respected. This belief forms the cornerstone of an operational Chinese company, its management, and its organizational structure.[24]

Currently, there are three prevalent forms of organizations in China: state-owned enterprises (SOEs), private firms, and joint-venture firms.

SOEs are owned by the national, local, or provincial government in China. These companies comprise China's major industries, such aerospace, shipbuilding, petroleum, and telecommunications. SOEs tend to be monopolistic, and their operations and governance reflect government policies. Private firms, in contrast, have a hierarchical structure that flows from owners to managers to workers. Joint-venture firms differ in that they usually operate independently from the parent organization that contributed the resources necessary for the formation of the joint venture.[25] However, in some instances, one or both of the parent companies may want to exercise managerial control.

Management Résumés

In our experience, a great many résumés in China contain misrepresentations, with the most frequent inaccuracy involving changing the dates of employment to cover up large gaps of time between jobs. In addition, we've found that approximately two-thirds of applicants' résumés embellish their employment position or list a position with a small company that is now out of business, making it difficult to verify the position claimed.

Another common inaccuracy on résumés involves an applicant claiming a bachelor's degree from a Chinese university when, in reality, the individual has only obtained a graduation certificate. A graduation certificate is received for obtaining the necessary credits to graduate, whereas a bachelor's degree requires the student to meet a higher set of standards.

We never to assume the data in a Chinese résumé is accurate unless each fact is independently verified. Many Chinese count on the fact that a shortage of qualified people for the position they're applying for will result in the company not verifying a majority of the data contained in their résumé. This is quite often the case, as many positions in a Chinese company go unfilled because of the lack of skilled personnel.

The increasing demand for skilled personnel has given rise to a rapid increase in fraudulent résumés.

Labor Relations

In order to perform forensic due diligence on the labor relations function of a Chinese company, one should first understand the emergence and role of labor rights and relations within a company. *Labor relations* refers to the social and economic relationship between the workers and their associated organizations.[26] Since the role of an individual worker is usually subordinate and passive, labor relations are most often collective, allowing for the views and preferences of workers within an organization.

The labor contract is the legal form for the establishment of individual labor relations. Labor relations contracts in China began to take hold in the mid-1980s and gained momentum, becoming mainstream in the 1990s. Chinese law stipulates that employers and employees shall establish labor relations contracts in accordance with the law and that the following requirements will be met:[27]

- Contracts shall be in writing.
- Contracts may or may not be for a fixed period of time.
- Contracts may or may not prescribe the work that's to be completed.
- Contracts shall strive for equality, voluntariness, and reaching unanimity through consultation.
- Trade union representatives, or other representatives empowered by the employees, may sign group contracts with the company.

Areas addressed in a labor contract include the following:

- labor remuneration
- working hours
- overtime pay
- bonus pay
- rest and vacation

- labor safety
- labor hygiene
- sick pay
- insurance
- welfare
- notice period
- dismissal

The government prohibits the hiring of people under the age of sixteen, as well as hiring women and minors (those between the ages of sixteen and eighteen) for tasks expressly prohibited by government regulations.[27]

The Labor Contract Law establishes the platform on which labor relations are based. This law influences labor relations in two complementary ways: it establishes effective labor standards by regulating an employer's obligations and securing labor rights that can be implemented under government supervision, and it fosters the formation of trade unions to allow workers to engage in collective bargaining with their employers.[26] Since the implementation of contract law in China, the All China Federation of Trade Unions (ACFTU) has placed an emphasis on the creation of trade unions within companies. The goal of these unions is to carry out collective negotiations.

In the first year after the implementation of the Labor Contract Law, labor dispute cases in Shanghai, for example, increased 199 percent from the previous year. Of these cases, 17 percent were decided in favor of the employer, a 5 percent increase from the previous year, suggesting an improving consciousness among employers with regard to labor relations. However, when an issue cannot be satisfactorily resolved, a work stoppage or slowdown may be the end result. In this case, the Trade Union Law of the People's Republic of China specifies that, if an enterprise or public institution is subject to a work stoppage or a slowdown, the union is required to represent trade employees in negotiations with the company.[26] The government, in this process, plays a neutral role, encouraging both parties to negotiate a settlement.

Employees who are unilaterally dismissed at the end of their fixed-term contract receive compensation in the amount of one month's salary for each year of service. The calculated monthly salary is based on the average monthly compensation received by the employee in the previous twelve months and includes bonuses and other allowances. The amount received by the employee is capped at 300 percent of the average salary for the city in which the employee works. The calculation for the years of service commences from January 1, 2008, when the Labor Contract Law was implemented.

Employees who are terminated for no valid reason are entitled to twice the amount of their compensation. However, this law is commonly misunderstood. Article 87 of the Labor Contract Law states that, even if the employer violates the law, it is still only liable for the double compensation specified in Article 47. Many employers seeking to terminate employees with a lesser amount of severance pay have used this as justification for paying a lower amount. However, an employee can demand continued performance of the employer under his employee contract as stipulated in Article 48. If the employee doesn't demand continued performance, the company will likely only pay the employee the double compensation.

Employee terminations is one of the areas we look at closely, as improper termination and nonpayment of required severance could result in corporate liabilities.[28] These liabilities might include the following:

- payment of an employee's salary for the remainder of the contract without a limitation of 300 percent of the average salary in the city in which the employee works.
- stipulated compensation at the end of the contract term
- court costs

Employees versus Independent Contractors

Many companies have turned to independent contractors as a way to contain labor costs. However, under Chinese Employee Contract Law, there's no *independent contractor* concept. Only two relationships are recognized: an employment relationship and a labor service relationship. Consequently, employers try to decrease their labor costs by establishing labor service relationships, for which they're not required to pay work-related costs like social security, work-related injury insurance, severance payments, and other fees associated with an employment agreement.[29]

Employment relationships are governed by labor law, whereas labor service relationships are covered by the civil code and contract law. When conducting our forensic due diligence, especially in an economic downturn, we see companies that actively employ "service" personnel in positions where there's clearly an employee function. There's no employment contract for these service workers, and obviously, none of the mandated fees required for an employee are paid by the company or the individual performing the corporate task. There's also generally less, and possibly no, severance pay associated with the termination of a service contract.

Chinese companies frequently utilize employment agencies when hiring personnel. Article 66 of the Labor Contract Law specifies that only temporary, substitute, or auxiliary positions should be filled through employment agencies.[28] However, the government has not clarified the definition of these positions, and many companies take advantage of this ambiguity to utilize employment agencies to fill company positions.

Chinese law also designates that if a contract with a full-time employee is not signed within one month of the employee commencing work, the employer must pay double the monthly salary per month to the employee commencing from the second month.[29] A domestic helper is not considered an employee of a family or individual.

Compensation Policy

An effective compensation policy usually addresses the following four objectives:[30]

1. Legal compliance
2. Cost-effectiveness
3. Internal, external, and individual equity for employees
4. Performance enhancement for the organization

There are a number of components contained within a corporation's compensation policy:

- direct pay
- base pay
- variable pay
    - bonuses
    - incentives
    - stock options
- indirect pay
- benefits
    - health insurance
    - paid time off
    - retirement pensions
- legal constraints
    - Labor Law of the People's Republic of China (1994)
    - Labor Contract Law of the People's Republic of China (2007)
    - Labor Arbitration and Dispute Resolution Law of the People's Republic of China (2007) and Labor Arbitration Law (2008)
    - Trade Union Law of the People's Republic of China (1994)

Since living standards vary in different parts of China, the central government has given the task of setting a minimum wage to the local government. The central government has made a statement that it wants to increase the minimum wage within China by 13 percent per year through 2015. When examining the company's payroll, you should compare the wages of employees to the minimum wage standards in the city or province in which the company is located to determine if standards are being adhered to.

The government has also issued standards for overtime pay. The standard working day in China is considered to be eight hours, with forty hours per week established as the standard work week. Saturday and Sunday are considered to be rest days. Employees who work longer than eight hours per day must be compensated at 150 percent of standard wages. In addition, employees who work on their designated rest days must be compensated at 200 percent of their standard wages or have their rest days switched.[30] Employees who are required to work on holidays must be compensated at 300 percent of their standard wage.

The government also mandates a package of benefits that employers are obligated to provide employees, including the following:

- retirement insurance (pension)
- medical insurance
- unemployment insurance.
- maternity insurance.
- work-related injury insurance.

Retirement insurance, medical insurance, and unemployment insurance are funded by a joint contribution from both the employee and employer.

Stock Compensation Plans

According to PricewaterhouseCoopers, an equity-based compensation plan—such as an employee share option plan (ESOP), employee share award plan (ESAP), and employee share purchase plan (ESPP)—is becoming a regular feature in an employee's remuneration package.[31] Many companies are recognizing the value of these plans, in times of economic boom as well as economic downturn, in locking employees into the company on a cost-effective basis. Moreover, according to Deloitte, equity-based compensation is used to do the following:[32]

- align employee and owner's interest
- allow for employee wealth creation
- encourage long-term commitment
- elicit specific performance objectives

However, only 51 percent of companies have registered their stock plan with the local tax bureau as required under Circular 35.

China's securities regulator, China Securities Regulatory Commission (CSRC), in a draft regulation, allows listed firms to buy their own shares on the secondary market through an asset management agency with a designated portion of their employee's cash compensation. Employees can voluntarily participate, according to the regulation, and receive shares according to a defined distribution agreement. However, the funds drawn from an individual worker should be no more than 30 percent of the compensation received in the past twelve months, including salary and bonus. In addition, the funds drawn should be less than one-third of the financial assets of the employee's family, and the shares must be held for at least thirty-six months.

The company's ESOP plan can hold no more than 10 percent of the shares of a listed company, and an individual worker cannot own more than one percent of the shares.[33] Corporate ESOP funds must be managed by an independent asset manager.

Employee Handbooks

Chinese labor laws require that all employers produce an employment handbook so that both the employer and the employee know their rights and obligations.[34] The handbook should focus on two areas: implementation of the labor laws and specific employee obligations.

Implementation of Labor Laws

Implementation of labor laws should address such areas as deception; competency; illness and injury; changing circumstances; and rule violations. Labor laws allow an employment contract to be voided if one party deceives the other, such as an employee providing a fake education certificate or a false qualification document. An employment handbook, providing guidelines as to what constitutes deception, has proved very effective in court and in labor arbitration cases.

It should also be noted that *changing circumstances*, as specified in the labor law, is a basis on which an employment contract may be terminated. This means that the circumstances on which the employment contract is based are no longer applicable and the defined services can no longer be performed.[34] There is an assumption that both parties have failed to negotiate a satisfactory alternative contract.

Termination of an employment contract for *rule violations*, as defined in the employment handbook, could be due to an employee violating corporate policy by downloading videos, accepting gifts from the firm's vendors, or using a corporate computer for non-work-related purposes.

Employee Obligations

The employment handbook defines employee obligations. These obligations cannot conflict with labor laws.

Related-Party Transactions

When performing a due diligence review of a Chinese company, it's vital to understand the various types of related-party transactions that are common in most Chinese businesses. This is especially important when the company is planning to become, or already is, publicly listed in the US, because the US Securities and Exchange Commission (SEC) requires full disclosure of such transactions.

In China, it's not uncommon for the chairman of a company to have the majority equity position. It's also not uncommon for him to intermingle his personal and business finances. This practice frequently leads to complications when outside investors are brought in, especially if the investment involves a public listing and the resulting requirement for transparency in financial reporting.

One of the most common related-party transactions we encounter is loans to and from officers of the company, involving the chairman in particular. There are varying reasons for these loans. For example, an officer of the company may be using the company's working capital as a personal bank account. In this scenario, the officer takes a low- or no-interest loan from the company and then reloans the money at a substantially higher rate of interest. Another possibility is that the corporate officer spends the money knowing that the rate of interest from the company, if any, will be lower than can be obtained from a bank. Where the company is in need of working capital, an officer may loan money to the company to give it quick access to capital without the necessity of going through the bank loan process.

Related-party loans are usually relatively simple transactions and are not always problematic. This is because they're frequently done for legitimate corporate purposes. However, problems arise when the company is publicly listed or intends to become so. Since the implementation of the Sarbanes Oxley Act of 2002, public companies are prohibited from making personal loans to officers or directors. As a result, these loans must be taken off the books prior to the company becoming public. Furthermore, loans from related parties that are made at no interest or at below-market interest rates may require special accounting procedures where market-level interest is imputed on the loan. This reduces profitability.

Another common type of related-party transaction is the use of personal bank accounts of directors or officers—and sometimes even lower-level employees at the direction of senior management—to transact corporate business. The purpose of utilizing personal accounts is most often to avoid the payment of taxes. For example, the company may instruct a customer to pay for goods by means of a wire transfer to the personal account of the chairman. In this instance, the company does not declare this sale for VAT and/or income tax purposes. The cash receipt does not show up in the corporate account, which may be subject to audit by the tax authorities. However, when it comes time to perform a US GAAP (generally accepted accounting principles) audit, this type of transaction is problematic because the company must either present books excluding the entire sale—since it does not have proper supporting documentation like a cash receipt on the bank statement or a VAT invoice to show the auditors—or it must allow the auditors access to the officer's personal bank account. In many cases, these accounts have intentionally been closed to muddy the paper trail, or the officer does not want to allow access to personal banking records. The investigator should ascertain early in the process whether collections or payments are made through personal bank accounts and, if so, whether such records will be available.

A third common related-party transaction involves dealings with suppliers or customers owned by officers or directors, or their immediate family members. Often, these transactions are legitimate and are conducted at arm's length. They're not problematic in and of themselves as long as they're fully disclosed. However, there are similar types of related-party transactions that can be very dangerous. The most egregious is the creation of fake customers or suppliers with which the company transacts business for the purposes of hiding fraud. These entities are created by management—or by family members or related parties—to accept payments from or make payments to the company resulting from bogus paper transactions designed to create a false financial picture. Chapter 11, "Independent Procedures," outlines some of the steps that can be taken to identify these types of fraudulent entities.

Off-Balance-Sheet Transactions

Off-balance-sheet transactions are a form of financing in which large capital expenditures are kept off a company's balance sheet through various classification methods.[35] Off-balance-sheet transactions are used for several reasons, including the ability to manage cash flow by keeping ownership of a capital asset with a separate entity and only paying for a lease or rent on the portion used. Companies also often use off-balance-sheet financing to keep their debt to equity (D/E) and leverage ratios low, especially if the inclusion of a large expenditure would break negative debt covenants.

One common form of an off-balance-sheet transaction is a capital lease, whereby a company leases capital assets from a third party but does not take ownership of the asset or incur a liability related to the full cost of the asset. Under US GAAP, these types of leases must generally be recorded on the lessee's balance sheet if the total payments relative to the value of the assets exceeds a certain threshold, generally 75 percent. Other types of off-balance-sheet financing include accounts receivable factoring agreements and bank lines of credit.

Off-balance-sheet transactions can also be used for financial manipulation. Enron, for example, notoriously used off-balance-sheet transactions to overstate its income and understate its debt. It did this by placing liabilities in special-purpose entities and joint ventures that were not consolidated into Enron's reported financial statements. US GAAP now requires a thorough analysis of possibly related off-balance-sheet enterprises, called *variable interest entities*, through the application of the FASB (Financial Accounting Standards Board) Interpretation No. (FIN) 46, "Consolidation of Variable Interest Entities."

FIN 46 requires a company to consolidate a variable-interest entity into its financial statements, if the reporting entity is the primary beneficiary of the variable-interest entity, and to include certain disclosures in the consolidated financial statements about the variable interest entity. This consolidation is required even if the reporting company is not a majority equity-holder of the variable-interest entity and is more dependent on qualitative factors. These factors include who ultimately absorbs the losses of the variable-interest entity, who has decision-making authority, and what the intent was in the design of the variable-interest entity. This can often be a contentious analysis with the audit firm and lead to an uncertain determination or outcome. Therefore, any entities of this type should be identified early in the process and the consolidation requirements analyzed in detail pursuant to the applicable accounting regulations.

Chapter 7

Financial Due Diligence in China

Performing financial due diligence in China can be vastly different from performing the same task in the US. Knowing where to look for common red flags in a Chinese accounting environment is essential.

In the Western world, reviewing financial information is often the first thing one does when evaluating a company. Evaluators want to first understand facts like the amount of sales and income for the past several years, profit margins, debt burden, collection times for accounts receivable, projected sales and income, and many other facts that can be gleaned from a reasonably complete and accurate set of financial statements. In China, however, most companies maintain at least three sets of books: one for the tax authorities, one for external reporting or investors, and one for banking institutions, if the company is a borrower. It's critical that those evaluating a Chinese company understand the financial information they're looking at, why it was prepared the way it was, and whether it should be relied upon as presented (hint: probably not).

At the start of an engagement, we ask the company to provide us with the following information:

- financial statements
- ledger details
- financial projections

- debt structure
- summary of tax policies
- copies of tax filings
- revenue and cost detail
- description of internal controls

These items provide the basis for analyzing the state of the entity's financial information. This is different from verifying that the financial information is correct. Rather, these items allow us to make a high-level determination of the accounting practices used to construct the financial statements—and to quickly identify where there may be fundamental problems with the presentation, such as under-reported tax liabilities, over-reported sales, or unrealistic cash balances.

Additional detailed procedures are required to analyze and conclude if the financial statements are indeed misstated or improperly prepared. Most of these procedures involve independent confirmation of the items in question, whether tax payments, cash balances, sales, purchases, or other items. These procedures are explained in detail in chapter 11.

Described below are some of the basic procedures and tools we employ to analyze a company's financial information and to determine what additional analytical detail is required.

Financial Statements

Internally generated financial statements, often referred to collectively as *management accounts*, are usually the first financial items we review. In China, management accounts typically consist of a balance sheet and an income statement. It's uncommon for Chinese management accounts to contain a statement of cash flow or shareholder equity, as is commonly the case in the West.

Identifying certain accounting methodologies and red flags in management accounts can provide critical guidance as to where more detailed procedures should be performed in a forensic due diligence review in order to uncover potential problem areas.

The initial review of management accounts varies according to the size of the company, the industry, the corporate structure, and other related factors. As a result, we tailor our review of management accounts for every company on which we preform forensic due diligence. A smartly executed review of the management accounts can identify some very obvious problems, as well as issues that may not be obvious to someone not accustomed to dealing with Chinese accounting practices. Below are some of the most common review procedures that we perform on management accounts.

Mathematical Checks

It may seem obvious, but the first thing we do when we receive the company's financial statement is make sure there are no calculation errors.

- We begin by footing down both the balance sheet and the income statement to make sure all totals are correct.
- We make sure that the balance sheet balances—that is, that total assets are equal to the sum of liabilities and shareholders' equity.
- We ensure that retained earnings roll forward. By the nature of double-entry accounting, the opening balance of retained earnings (the balance at the end of the previous fiscal year) plus the current year's net income, less any dividend distributions, should be equal to the current year's retained earnings—in the absence of any journal entries directly to retained earnings, which, using proper accounting standards, should be rare. It's not uncommon to find that these numbers do not add up for private Chinese companies. One inconsistency we've encountered is that companies will move income or expenses between fiscal years in order to manage earnings—for example, moving sales made late in the previous year to the current year to inflate current-year sales and income. The discrepancy could also be caused by a fundamental problem with the company's accounting practices. Whatever the reason, if retained earnings do not roll forward, the problem should be addressed in additional detail to determine the underlying cause.

Balance Sheet

- The face of the balance sheet can tell quite a bit about the integrity of the financial statement and also identify areas that call for a more in-depth investigation.
- All roads lead to cash. That's to say that nearly every fraud, misstatement, error, or other problem with a Chinese financial statement in some way affects or flows through cash. Bogus sales must eventually be monetized, or they will be discovered. Underreported taxable income must be reconciled to cash in the bank. Fixed assets and inventory must be paid for in cash. For these reasons, the most meaningful procedures we perform in forensic due diligence relate in some way to cash. These procedures include independently obtaining bank statements to verify cash balances and tracing customer collections; inventory and fixed asset purchases; bank loans; tax payments; and many other items related to bank statements. These independent procedures are outlined in further detail in chapter 11.
- On the face of the balance sheet, we look at the cash balance and initially analyze it relative to the other financial accounts and the facts and circumstances of the company, its industry, its business model, its financing transactions, and other relevant facts and circumstances. Questions we might ask include the following:
    - Are they are reinvesting all of their profits, so one would expect a low cash balance?
    - Is their cash tied up in plants and equipment and other real assets?
    - Do they have seasonal sales or collections that would affect cash as of the balance sheet date?
    - Are they required to carry substantial amounts of inventory ahead of sales?
    - What are their debt balances?

Each situation is different, and we are simply looking to see if the cash balance seems reasonable considering all of the known facts.

- One area we typically focus on is the aging of accounts receivable (AR). Before examining detailed schedules, such as an AR listing, we look at the estimated age of outstanding accounts by dividing the AR balance by average daily sales (taken as the annual sales from the income statement divided by 365). The quotient tells us approximately how many days' worth of sales is in the account as of the balance sheet date. This can be compared to the expected collection cycle based on the company's industry and other business attributes.
- In our experience, collection cycles tend to be longer in China, just as a matter of historical business culture. If the company also makes a substantial amount of sales to state-owned enterprises, the collection cycles may be even longer, since the government is a notoriously slow payer. However, an unusually high number of days' sales in AR could indicate that the company is inflating its sales figures by booking fictional sales that it never made or will never actually collect on.

  Because this metric is based on the total year's average daily sales as compared with a snapshot of AR on a particular date, it's not an exact measure. As a result, it should not be taken as a definitive indicator of any underlying problems, only as a useful tool in identifying potential concerns and guiding your investigation in the right direction.
- Similar to AR, the aging of a company's inventory can be calculated using the inventory balance divided by the average daily cost of sales. This calculation reflects the approximate age of the company's inventory. An unusually high number relative to industry benchmarks could indicate that the company has slow-moving or obsolete inventory that it may never be able to monetize, indicating that this amount may need to be written down. For a company in an inventory-centric

business, unusually low balances relative to sales could indicate that sales were booked, and inventories reduced accordingly, prior to the balance-sheet date to inflate the current-year earnings. There are no definitive rules when it comes to analyzing this data. What we're looking for are facts that differ from expectations, indicating that the account needs to be examined in further detail.

- Look at the size of other accounts receivable (other AR). Other AR is a catch-all balance-sheet holding account used by many Chinese companies. Often, this account represents a substantial portion, and in some cases even a majority, of total assets. In our experience, most of the items classified as Other AR should either be classified elsewhere or, more importantly for the purposes of financial reporting and enterprise valuation, charged to the income statement before the balance-sheet date. If this account is material, we'll ask the company to provide a reconciliation of each item showing beginning balance, debits, credits, and an ending balance that agrees with the balance sheet. The following are some of the most common items that we see in Other AR:
    - *basic expenses like utilities, market costs, and other operating expenses that have been incurred and paid, but for which the vendor has not issued an invoice.* Companies tend to hold these expenses in Other AR until the invoice is received, at which time it will be recognized and matched with the tax books, since the tax deduction cannot be taken without the invoice. However, for GAAP (generally accepted accounting principles) reporting, the expense should be recognized when incurred.
    - *inventory purchases* for which an invoice has not been received.
    - *loans to related parties,* such as the chairman and his family, directors, and employees. If the company is going public in the US, for example, these types of loans will be prohibited by the Sarbanes–Oxley Act of 2002 (SOX).

- *shadow-banking loans to unrelated parties*, where the company acts as an unauthorized lending agent and charges premium interest rates. *Shadow banking* is a term used for nonbank financial intermediaries who perform services similar to a commercial bank. These intermediaries do not have banking licenses and do not take deposits. They simply act as intermediaries between investors and borrowers and make their money from either a fee or the interest-rate spread between what it pays the investor and what it receives from the borrower. These loans violate Chinese government lending regulations, which could require accrual or disclosure of penalties and/ or interest if the company becomes subject to US GAAP.
- *deposits against land-use rights* or fixed assets that should be categorized as long term assets.
- *intercompany accounts* that should be reclassified to a separate intercompany elimination account.

- We look at the amount of debt the company is carrying relative to its equity and its assets. If a company has a material amount of debt, we'll perform additional procedures related to the debt, including analyzing the terms of the debt, confirming debt directly with the bank, verifying that interest expense is reasonable relative to debt amounts and applicable interest rates, and other procedures as required.
- Similar to Other AR, many Chinese companies maintain a generic liability account to capture items that should be classified elsewhere or charged to income. This account is usually called other accounts payable (Other AP). Items commonly reflected in Other AP include:

  - *loans from related parties*, such as the chairman and his family, directors, and employees. These loans are often made to companies that have maxed out their lending ability from commercial banks, do not have credit to get a loan from a commercial bank, or operate in an industry for which lending has been halted by the Chinese government. Even if they are interest-free, such loans may require imputed interest expense to be charged to the income statement under US GAAP. If the company is going public in the US, these types of loans will also be prohibited by SOX.
  - *shadow-banking loans from unrelated parties*, where the other party acts as an unauthorized lending agent and charges premium interest rates. These types of loans are usually taken by companies that have either maxed out their lending ability from commercial banks, do not have credit to get a loan from a commercial bank, or operate in an industry for which lending has been halted by the Chinese government. If such loans exist, it's important to look for a corresponding interest expense on the income statement.
  - intercompany accounts that should be reclassified to a separate intercompany elimination account.
- We always look to see if the company has any accrued income tax liabilities. Taken in context with the company's applicable tax rates and policies, purported financial results, and tax forms and payments, we can form a reasonable expectation of whether a liability should be reflected, and then check to see if it is.

Income Statement

- As with the balance sheet, we can identify potential problem areas and accounts that could require additional investigation by performing a few quick checks of the income statement.
- We check to see if profit margins are reasonable for the company's industry and if margins have fluctuated materially between quarterly or annual periods.
- We compare overhead expenses to sales and ascertain whether the percentage is reasonable relative to comparable companies.
- We check that interest expense is reasonable compared with debt balances and applicable interest rates. It's common for Chinese companies to record interest expense on a cash basis when it's withdrawn by the bank rather than accruing interest as required by GAAP.
- We look at income tax expense as compared to pretax income and reconcile this to what we know about the company's taxation policies. For example, if a company is an ordinary taxpayer, we would expect income tax to be 25 percent of pretax income, or at least close enough that we can separately reconcile the differences between tax and book income. If a company has no income tax expense, we would examine the basis for its tax exemption in further detail.
- If the company has other notable income or expense items, we would want to inspect these. Examples could include the following:
    - subsidies, which we would reconcile to existing documentation and bank receipts, and confirm with the subsidizing government agency
    - scrap sales, which we would test for reasonableness based on the company's manufacturing process and/or confirm with customers
    - investment income, which we could validate through bank statements, contracts, and independent confirmation

Cash Flow Statement

Although it's uncommon for Chinese companies to prepare a US-style statement of cash flow as part of their management accounts, it's often beneficial for the party performing the due diligence to prepare such a statement.

The cash flow statement indicates how much cash was used during the accounting period and what it was used for. A typical cash flow statement is divided into three categories: cash provided by/used in operating activities, investing activities, and financing activities.

The most common form of cash flow statement reconciles net income to cash generated or used. It does this by adding back noncash transactions to net income; reflecting changes in the operating balance-sheet accounts; showing capital expenditures that are not reflected as expense in the income statement and adding financing transactions like a loan or equity activity. In essence, the cash flow statement ties together the activity on the income statement with the financial positions on the balance sheet to show how cash was affected by the company's business activity.

Preparing a comprehensive cash flow statement requires access to accounting records more detailed than a summary balance sheet or income statement. With cooperation from the company, it's a fairly simple exercise. Nevertheless, even without access to the full records of the company, a rough version can still be prepared that will provide the evaluator with useful insights.

Ledger Detail

A high-level review of the general ledger detail may provide evidence of accounting areas that could require a more in-depth analysis.

In addition to reviewing the summary-level financial statements, we also ask each of the company's entities to provide us with account-level financial information printed from their general ledger software. This allows us to look more closely at the activity within key accounts and make some basic determinations about the reliability of the financial statements.

Common checks and balances we perform to make sure that basic accounting principles are applied to the financial statements include the following:

- Compare aggregated debits in cash to total sales, and credits in cash to total charges on the income statement (cost of goods sold plus expenses). These amounts should not be exactly the same for multiple reasons, including noncash charges to the income statement, such as depreciation and amortization; changes in current assets and liabilities for items like revenue recognized but not collected or accrued expenses not yet paid; or cash received in debt or equity financing transactions. However, the total cash recorded in and out of the bank accounts should be readily reconcilable to the income statement. This is, in essence, how a statement of cash flow works.

  As an example, we once performed a review where the company's annual sales were in the range of 200–300 million yuan, but total debits and credits in the cash accounts totaled over a billion yuan on each side. Even taking debt and noncash items into account, this was an easily recognizable red flag. We noted substantial transfers by the company between accounts at different banks. After investigating with company management and bank officials, we concluded that the company was moving cash in order to increase cash activity on the bank's ledger. Since cash activity was one of the primary criteria used by the bank for determining its ability to lend to a customer, this cash movement increased the company's borrowing power with the bank, and it was able to secure more loans than it would have otherwise.

This scheme was actually being executed at the recommendation of the bank manager, who was under pressure from his superiors to increase outgoing loans and thus maximize income on his available cash. However, he needed hard data to make sure the loans met with bank guidelines. The company benefitted by receiving additional capital and also by strengthening business and personal ties with the bank manager.

This was one of those gray areas in China. It wasn't clear whether this was a violation of law or lending guidelines; the bank's lending criteria were being met even though rules were being bent for the benefit of both parties. However, it's important to understand the ramifications of these actions and that the company's true borrowing power may in fact be less than what's reflected on its financial statements.

- Compare debits in accounts receivable to sales. In the absence of a substantial amount of direct cash sales, these amounts should reconcile. Since cash sales are still fairly common in China, these amounts will often need to be reconciled to account for cash sales, but this is still a good way to identify manual adjustments to sales caused by moving sales to different periods after the fact in order reach a desired sales or income target.
- Compare credits in the finished-goods inventory account to cost of goods sold on the income statement. These amounts should agree or should be easily reconciled. If they are materially different, it could indicate either an underlying flaw in the inventory control process or material adjustments to cost of goods sold resulting from an after-the-fact reclassification of sales and related cost of goods.
- Compare credits in fixed assets and land-use-rights accounts to depreciation and amortization expenses. Credit to these accounts could include impairment or disposal transactions as well, which should be easily reconcilable.
- Check changes in equity accounts for reasonableness. This includes making sure that the change in retained earnings

equals net income for the period and that any dividends or profit distributions are properly recorded in retained earnings. Also, any equity-financing transactions should be properly reflected in the capital accounts.

We maintain a copy of the ledger detail and will refer back to it from time to time when performing other procedures. For example, if we are verifying fixed assets, we'll check whether any fixed-asset purchases were properly recorded at cost in the ledger. If we are verifying cash, we will reconcile the ending balance of each account to its corresponding sub-ledger account. If we are verifying tax payments, we will trace the payment out to the cash ledger. A large portion of the tests we perform end up with a confirmation back to the corresponding entry in the general ledger.

Projections

Financial projections are not a representation of past verifiable facts but rather an estimate of future performance based on assumptions about expected performance. They cannot be definitively proven or disproven, but there is still plenty of diligence that can be performed on projections to give the users comfort that they're at least rational and logical.

Assuming a relatively simple manufacturing or distribution operation and recognizing that each company and industry has its own unique set of assumptions, procedures we might perform on projected financial information include the following:

- Verify that the assumption of units shipped is reasonable when compared to prior actual results.
- Review pricing assumptions and verify that they're reasonable when compared to historical pricing as well as industry pricing.
- Review gross profit margins relative to historical results.
- Review components of overhead and marketing expenses relative to historical results.

- Ensure that income tax rate assumptions are accurate relative to the company's actual government-mandated tax policies, including expiration of any tax incentives currently in place.
- Stress-test the model by using a reasonable range for each material assumption and observing the impact on the financial results.

Of course, market trends, macroeconomics, microeconomics, competitors, and a multitude of subjective factors can have a dramatic impact on projections, As a result, we take a more consultative view of these items. From the viewpoint of factual verification, the procedures we perform on projected financial information is somewhat limited, and this data is primarily used to provide context for examination of historical transactions and events.

Debt Agreements

Understanding a company's debt structure means more than just reviewing a list of outstanding loans. To perform meaningful forensic due diligence on a Chinese company's debt, the unique characteristics of this type of borrowing must be taken into consideration.

The review process should start with a list of outstanding loans, including for each the lending institution's name and branch location, loan inception date, loan maturity date, applicable interest rate, description of security provided, and any other relevant features of these instruments. Next, obtain copies from the company of each debt arrangement, including the security agreement with the bank and any appraisal or valuation reports related to the underlying security.

Issues we look for when examining the documentation include the following:

- *Does the bank documentation appear legitimate?* This seems basic, but we have been provided with falsified bank documentation. It's advisable to independently, and directly, confirm any domestic bank loans in China with an in-person visit to the bank.

- *Who owns the underlying security?* It's not uncommon for Chinese companies to borrow from a bank using the assets of another person or entity as security. The other entity may be a relative of one of the company's principal shareholders, a key customer or supplier who depends on the business of the company, or an unrelated party who "lends" assets as security for a fee or other consideration. If another party owns the underlying security, verify that these assets are not recorded on the company's books. Also, if the third party is charging a fee for the use of the assets to secure a loan, be sure that these charges are recorded on the company's income statement.
- *Is the valuation or appraisal report reliable?* We've seen valuation reports prepared by local Chinese firms that are far less thorough, logical, and reliable than their Western counterparts. We typically compare the asset's appraised value to the carrying value for reasonableness. If the values are materially different, we attempt to determine why.

  In some cases, the valuator overvalues the assets in order to increase the amount that the company may borrow or to meet minimum borrowing requirements. This is often done with the unofficial consent of the bank's loan officer and creates an inherent risk for the bank. Therefore, if the asset is overvalued and the bank has to foreclose, the value realized will be less than the amount of the loan.

  In other circumstances, we've seen companies that pledge the assets of other people or entities, sometimes related and sometimes not, as collateral for their bank loans. The borrowing entity will borrow money from the bank using the third party's assets as collateral. In accomplishing this, they will utilize a collateral agreement at the prevailing bank interest rate. It's in writing, and the bank is aware of it. The borrowing entity will then turn around and loan the money to the third party at a higher rate. This type of transaction is usually done when the third party does not have sufficient credit to borrow from the bank or its borrowing limit is too low. In these cases, there's a more direct impact on the borrower in that, if the value of the third party's assets is overstated, the borrower could have exposure.

In other words, if the third party does not repay the borrower and the borrower allows the bank to foreclose on the assets, the bank could still have a claim against the borrower for the difference between the amount realized from the liquidation of the assets and the loan amount. If the asset value is materially overstated, the exposure of the company could be material. This could result in an adjustment to the carrying value of the loan receivable from the third party, which would negatively impact earnings.

- *Is the lending institution a government-authorized lending agent?* As we've discussed, shadow banking is a huge industry in China and a common source of funding for small and medium enterprises. These types of lending arrangements contravene Chinese government lending regulations. While this is certainly worth noting for the examining party, it's a common practice in China and generally overlooked by the government. But if the company is being, or has been, audited for the purpose of publishing financials or to file with a regulatory body if and when they complete a transaction, there are financial-statement implications to these types of loans.

  These implications are often overlooked and can lead to future restatements or misrepresentation claims. It should be noted that if a company is partaking in these types of loans, they should at the least disclose and record a contingent liability related to penalties and fines that could be imposed by the Chinese government for violation of lending regulations. In addition, in many cases we've found that companies do not record interest expense related to these loans, which are often done with no documentation between the officers of the lending and borrowing institutions. As a result, there's no paper trail, either for purposes of the lending violation or for the recording of interest by both parties. The lender does not want to claim taxable income, so interest payments will often be paid from personal account to personal account outside the records of the respective companies. Likewise, the borrower will not show an interest expense.

Under US GAAP, even if the consideration paid by a borrower to a lender is not cash-based, the borrower is in most cases required to record the fair value of the consideration received. Loans received with no consideration given, and which have no business reason, are likely to draw the attention of regulators. As a result, in cases where these loans exist, we examine the accounting treatment of interest related thereto.

Taxation

It's no secret that issues related to taxation have been the source of many failed investments in China. It's nearly impossible to perform financial due diligence of any value without understanding the Chinese taxation system and how to analyze the risks associated with taxation.

Before discussing specific documentation required by China's taxing authorities, it's important to have an understanding of China's system of taxation. A separate system was established in China in 1994 with both the Ministry of Finance and the State Tax Bureau in charge.[36] However, the two organizations have separate responsibilities. The State Tax Bureau is responsible for tax administration, while the Ministry of Finance is in charge of collecting taxes through two distinct bureaus: the tax bureau and customs.

Corporate Income Tax

The new Corporate Income Tax (CIT) Law of the People's Republic of China became effective in January 2008. The general provision of this law created a standard CIT rate of 25 percent, applicable both to resident and nonresident enterprises. The law also established a reduced CIT rate of 15 percent applicable to certain advanced and new technology enterprises designated by the government.

Taxes Levied on Foreign Investment Enterprise

Foreign Investment Enterprises (FIEs) are taxed at a rate of 30 percent. This tax is due when the FIE engages in business operations or production in China. If the FIE has no business operations in China but derives income from sources within the country, the company must pay a withholding tax of 20 percent on such income. Local income tax is computed on taxable income at a rate of 3 percent. Special economic zones and economic and technological development zones may have tax exemptions or provide for a reduction of the income tax. FIEs with headquarters in China may avoid double taxation through the use of a foreign tax credit for income tax paid abroad. China has signed double taxation agreements with forty-six countries. Foreign tax credits can be carried forward for up to five years.

Other Business Taxes

- *Value-added tax (VAT)*, which has three tiers:
    - a 17 percent tax applicable to all taxpayers selling or importing goods as well as those providing processing services, replacement, and repairs
    - a 13 percent tax applicable to all taxpayers selling or importing grains, edible vegetable oil, coal gas, natural gas, coals or charcoal products for household use, books, newspapers, magazines, chemical fertilizers, agricultural chemicals, and agricultural machinery
    - no tax for taxpayers exporting goods; having taxable labor services with an annual sales volume under 1 million yuan; engaged in wholesale or retail operations with an annual sales volume of less than 1.8 million yuan; or who the tax authority designates as a small VAT payer where the tax rate is 6 percent on a tax-in-price basis

- *Excise tax* that the producer or seller pays to the government for particular types of products. The seller would then try to recover this tax by adding the amount of the tax on to the cost of the goods they sell.
- *Business tax* that can range from 9 to 20 percent on specific taxable items.
- *Individual inc*ome tax on wages and salaries with nine progressive levels, ranging from 5 to 45 percent. Taxable income is considered income from wages and salaries; income from a production or business operation derived by an individual industrial or commercial household; income from a contracted or leased operation of enterprises or institutions; income from authors' or personal service remuneration; income from royalties; income from interest; interest from dividends; interest from bonuses; income from the lease or transfer of property; and other income as specified by the Ministry of Finance.
    - For foreign taxpayers, there's a monthly deduction of 4,000 yuan; for domestic employees, 840 yuan. Income from royalties, personal services, interest, dividends, bonuses, property leases, transfer of property, and contingent income shall be taxed at 20 percent.
    - The definition of a taxpayer is fairly broad in China. Besides domestic Chinese citizens, it includes individuals who are not domiciled in China, who have been domiciled, or who have resided in China for less than a year but derive their income from within China. There are more complex definitions of a taxpayer based on the length of domicile or residency within China and whether income is derived from within or from outside of China.
    - A tax year is normally a calendar year unless a foreign enterprise can demonstrate to the tax authorities that it has difficulties in computing its taxable income on a calendar-year basis.

Property Taxes

There are currently five types of property taxes levied on land-related property at various stages in the sales process:[37]

1. Farmland occupation tax, levied at the land acquisition and transaction stage
2. Land value-added tax, levied at the land acquisition and transaction stage
3. Urban land-use tax, levied at the possession stage
4. Real estate tax, levied at the possession stage
5. Deed tax, levied when the ownership of the property is transferred

A land appreciation tax ranges from 30 to 60 percent. There are four progressive levels, depending on the amount of the land appreciation and the allowable deduction.

An urban real estate tax is levied on the owner or renter and consists of two parts: a tax on buildings, calculated at 1 percent of the building's price, and a 1.5 percent land tax, based on the price of the land. If it's difficult to separate the land and building price, a rate of 1.5 percent is used.

Real estate taxes are not levied on the assessed value of the property. Instead, they're levied on the original purchase price minus a 10 to 30 percent depreciation, at a rate of 1.2 percent of depreciation. For leased property, it's levied at 15 percent of the actual rental income for the leased property.

Vehicle Taxes

The vehicle tax, for both automobiles and vessels, changed on January 1, 2012. China's State Administration of Taxation (SAT) has designated that the new tax rates are based on the vehicle's seating capacity and engine size.[38] Electric and hybrid vehicles are tax exempt. The tax is 300 yuan per year to a maximum of 5,400 yuan per year for vehicles with engine sizes greater than 4,000cc.

Natural-Resource Taxes

Natural-resource taxes in China underwent a major reform on November 1, 2011. Beginning on that date, both crude oil and natural gas were taxed on sales rather than on the amount of production. This revised taxation imposed a tax of between 5 and 10 percent of the sales value. Prior to this date, crude oil was taxed at between eight and thirty yuan for each ton of crude oil, and between two and fifteen yuan for each cubic kilometer of natural gas. Foreign energy companies that engage in Sino–foreign cooperative onshore and offshore oil and gas explorations will be liable for the payment of resource taxes rather than royalties.

This change in natural-resource taxes does not apply to coal, rare earth, and nonferrous metal ore, which will remain volume based. Coking coal is taxed at a rate of between eight and twenty yuan per ton, with other types of coal taxed at between three and five yuan per ton. Nonferrous metals are taxed at between 0.4 and thirty yuan per ton, and rare earth ores are taxed at between 0.4 and sixty yuan per ton.[39] One reason for such a wide range of tax on rare earth ores is that heavy rare earth is scarcer and, therefore, subject to higher taxes.

Vessel Usage and Tonnage Tax

Vessel usage and tonnage tax is levied on specified vessels and administered by the State General Administration of Customs. The revenue from this tax goes directly to the central government. The tax for vessels is between 1.2 and 5 yuan per net tonnage for a motorized vessel and 0.6 to 1.4 yuan per deadweight tonnage for a nonmotorized vessel.[40]

A vessel tonnage tax is paid by the users or entrusted foreign agents of the following:

- foreign vessels entering a Chinese harbor
- Chinese vessel chartered to a foreign businessperson
- Chinese or foreign vessel used by a Chinese joint venture
- foreign vessel chartered to China and sailing overseas, or sailing overseas and engaged in domestic coastal trade

Chinese vessels transporting foreign goods by a one-way lease are exempt from this tax.[41] In addition, a tax exemption may apply to vessels used by the government or government agencies; military units; fishing vessels with a deadweight capacity of less than one ton; pontoons and floating docks used exclusively for passengers, the loading or unloading of cargo, or the storage of goods; and police, fire, health, or environmental vessels.[40]

Taxes levied by customs includes both import tariffs and export tariffs.[36]

Tax Procedures

Issues related to taxation spread across every aspect of the due diligence process. In chapter 11, we'll discuss in detail the processes we use to independently verify tax reporting and payments, and to reconcile amounts reported to the taxing authorities to amounts presented to investors. However, as a first step in the process, we ask that companies provide us with all documentation, formal and informal, related to their taxation policies and reporting. This includes tax registration certificates, tax returns submitted to the SAT, and any documentation related to tax exemptions, incentives, or holidays. We review this information to gain a basic understanding of the company's tax situation.

There are many recurring themes that we find related to taxation. Companies that are subject to a VAT often make sales to customers "under the table," meaning that the sale price is paid by the customer either in hard cash or through the personal bank account of a company employee or trusted party. The transaction is then not declared as a sale by the company on the VAT return that's filed with the government, thus reducing the company's tax liability. Off-the-books sales may also not be reported for income tax purposes, reducing the company's taxable income and related income tax liability.

Companies sometimes rely on an informal tax exemption from the local office of the SAT, although that office has no authority to issue such an exemption. In practice, the local tax office is responsible for collecting tax, and so it can enforce the collection as it sees fit. However, only the central government has the authority to issue an actual tax exemption. It's not uncommon for companies to receive informal tax exemption certificates or confirmation letters from the local tax office if an audit or due diligence review requires such a document. However, unless formally numbered and chopped by the central government, these documents are not valid pursuant to Chinese tax law.

Revenue and Cost Detail

When an evaluator is analyzing a company, particularly in a traditional manufacturing, distribution, or retail environment, a proper analysis of revenue, cost, and gross profit margin can provide valuable insights.

Gross profit margin is revenue less cost of goods sold, expressed as a percentage of revenue. As with most things in China, taking a company's representation of its profit margins at face value can be a serious mistake.

At the outset of a typical due diligence assignment, we ask the company to provide supporting details of the revenue and cost-of-goods-sold figures it reports, whether that reporting is internal or external. Issues we generally look for in Chinese companies with respect to gross profit margins include the following:

- *Profit margins relative to the industry*—Historical and projected profit margins should be analyzed against comparable companies, both in China and in other parts of the world. Some Chinese companies listed in the US have been subject to short-seller attacks focusing on unrealistic gross profit margins compared to competitors, both domestic and foreign. If a company has a true competitive cost advantage stemming from factors like proprietary manufacturing techniques, patent protection, a superior distribution channel, and lower overhead, that advantage should be corroborated, with the underlying data and tested for reasonableness.

- *Customer concentrations*—These should be examined to identify any material concentration risks that should be disclosed to the investing or buying party.
- *Cost methodology in the company's accounting for cost of goods sold*—These figures should be examined in detail, especially for a newly public Chinese company that's just being exposed to US GAAP. In our experience, cost recognition procedures for private Chinese companies are substantially less sophisticated than those of US public and privately held companies. The allocation of materials, labor, and plant overhead costs can be fairly complicated for a multifaceted manufacturing operation. And because the accounting can be somewhat subjective, cost recognition is an area where Chinese companies often attempt to manipulate earnings by moving costs between periods, or out of cost-of-goods-sold and into operating expenses to improve the gross profit margin.
- *The impact of inappropriate past VAT accounting on future margins*—Private Chinese companies often underreport sales in order to reduce tax liability. Aside from the historical VAT liability issues that can arise (see chapter 11, "Independent Procedures"), this can also have the effect of distorting gross profit margins. When a company is underreporting its revenue on its VAT returns, it's often doing so not only to lower its tax liability but also to compete with other companies that sell similar products free of VAT. In other words, all other things being equal, if the competitor down the road is selling the same

product but is not reporting its revenue for VAT purposes, it can sell the product to the customer at a discount compared to the company that reports all of its revenue to the government. The discount is equal to the VAT rate, which is usually 17 percent. If a company has historically not reported its revenue for VAT purposes and its now suddenly required to because of increased transparency requirements when becoming a public company, it may be forced to lower sale price or lose customers. Otherwise, customers may move to a competitor who does not markup goods for VAT. This transition can have a material adverse effect on the company's business and should be given due consideration.

Internal Controls

The quality of a company's internal controls can provide valuable guidance about where a financial due diligence review should be focused. On one hand, strong internal controls provide added comfort regarding the reliability of financial information prepared by the company's management. On the other hand, a weak internal control environment can be an indicator of fundamentally flawed financial data.

Internal controls are accounting processes and systems designed to accomplish an accounting goal, such as to promote efficiency in completing an accounting task, assure implementation of an accounting policy, safeguard corporate assets, or avoid financial reporting fraud or error. Public companies in the US must comply with SOX, which requires companies to perform an evaluation—under the supervision of its primary officers—of the effectiveness of internal controls over financial reporting. For larger companies, the evaluation must also be audited by their independent auditors.

In our experience, Chinese companies that list in the US tend to have a difficult time complying with SOX. There are several reasons for this. First, the concept of documenting and testing internal controls, as a task separate from the audit of the underlying results themselves, is foreign to most Chinese companies. Second, documented policies and procedures are uncommon in China, as they are not seen as critical to the core function of the business. Third, record-keeping in China tends to be much more manual and paper-oriented compared to that in the US. This makes the internal-control documentation and testing process much more cumbersome.

For Chinese companies that are already public, internal-control due diligence should focus on reviewing the documentation prepared by the company relating to its SOX internal control review. This should include the mapping of the critical functions of the business; risk-rating of controls and procedures that are in place; and documentation of the testing performed, with conclusions relating significant deficiencies and material weaknesses in the internal control structure. The company also would have published a description of the material weaknesses in its filings with the SEC.

The review should focus not only on the deficient and weak controls identified by the test work—and its potential impact on any transaction being contemplated—but also on the quality of the review performed by the company. In other words, was the review carried out in accordance with the requirements of SOX? Was due consideration given to critical controls? Were deficient control areas common to China—such as tax reporting, cash management, related party transactions, and management override—given proper consideration?

The internal-control review should not be taken at face value, especially for smaller companies for which an independent audit of the internal control evaluation is not required. For private Chinese companies considering going public in the US, the process can be much more involved. This is because there's usually been no analysis of internal controls performed and, accordingly, there's no prior documentation of how these controls interact and operate. The process must therefore be carried out from scratch, which can be time-consuming and expensive.

The level of due diligence to be performed will be dictated by the scope of the assignment, but at the very least, consideration should be given to controls that are present in the critical areas identified in this section. The controls that are in place in those areas can also provide guidance as to the amount and type of forensic due diligence that should be performed.

Chapter 8
Competition

Because of China's unique combination of free market enterprise and communist government control, the competitive landscape for a company operating in China requires special examination. In many ways, analyzing a Chinese company's position relative to its competitors is similar to what would be performed in the US or other Western countries. As a result, and due to the substantial free-market forces at work within China, it's a good idea to start with conventional Western analysis tools.

Specifically, as part of our standard forensic due diligence checklist, we ask our clients to prepare an analysis of their strengths, weaknesses, opportunities, and threats, commonly known as a SWOT analysis. A SWOT analysis is an assessment of the dynamics affecting a business both internally—considering the strengths and weaknesses of the company and its employees relative to its competitors—and externally—taking into account opportunities and threats in the competitive environment that may create an advantage or disadvantage.

This type of analysis is common in the Western world but much less so in China. While executives in China are likely evaluating their businesses by the same fundamental measurements used in a SWOT analysis, the exercise of putting the assessment on paper and formulating specific business strategies and processes around those factors is not widespread.

A properly prepared SWOT analysis can give a due diligence team not only a general understanding of the company's business but also guidance about which areas of the due diligence process may require a deeper analysis and investigation. However, in asking a Chinese company to prepare the SWOT analysis and in evaluating the results, it's necessary to take into consideration many factors applicable to doing business in China that may not be understood in the West.

Take, for example, the internal portion of the SWOT analysis, which involves analyzing strengths and weaknesses relative to competitors. Many of the same basic business advantages and disadvantages that can be found with US companies will also apply to companies in China. This includes the quality of human resources, physical assets, intellectual property, distribution channels, product reputation, funding, and financial metrics. However, there are a number of internal factors specific to operating in China that should be considered relative to other competitors. One common example relates to the payment of taxes. Companies commonly underreport the amount of sales made in order to reduce their value-added tax (VAT) liability and the amount of sales and pretax income achieved in order to reduce income tax liability.

This issue comes to the forefront when a Chinese company is looking to list on a foreign stock exchange, specifically one that requires financial statements that are prepared and audited in accordance with internationally accepted accounting and auditing principles. Aside from the issue of whether the company may have a large undeclared historical tax liability (discussed in detail in chapter 11), there's the business issue of whether the company can keep pace with its competitors once it goes straight.

When a Chinese company that has historically underreported its tax liabilities goes public, it will be required to correct this issue, since its auditors will almost certainly look closely at all tax matters. This fact can work against the company from a competitive perspective on two fronts.

First, all sales will have to be reported to the tax bureau on the company's VAT returns. In order to deduct all of the input costs against sales in accordance with Chinese tax law, the company will need to require all suppliers to issue formal invoices, including VAT, for all materials purchased by the company. For privately held Chinese companies, it's a common practice to purchase materials from a supplier under the table, with the materials paid for in cash or through a non-corporate bank account. the supplier does not issue a formal invoice or charge VAT. This allows the purchasing company to sell the product to its customer free of VAT and, therefore, at a much lower cost—usually 17 percent lower. This in turn means that the company will realize a reasonable margin on its product. If the company is required to pay VAT to its supplier, it must pass this additional tax on to its customer or eat the cost, eroding profitability. In a landscape with many private competitors, customers may be unwilling to pay the VAT-included price, as they're conditioned to doing business off the books. Instead of paying the VAT-included price, they'll simply look to a competitor who is not public and who can sell the product without the VAT. Accordingly, it's imperative to analyze a company's historical VAT practices and the impact that reporting all VAT could have on future sales and profitability levels.

Second, if a company is required to report all of its income to the government for the purpose of recognizing and paying income taxes, it will be at a competitive disadvantage to other privately held companies in its industry. This is because it will realize lower net profitability and cash flow relative to sales than its competitors. If a company is required to pay the standard 25 percent corporate income tax rate and its private competitors are declaring only a small portion of income and paying, for example, 5 percent of their true pretax income in the form of taxes, then all other things being equal the competitor has a distinct advantage. The competitor will generate more cash flow on equivalent sales which can be reinvested into marketing, expansion, new product development, and other growth opportunities.

From a due diligence perspective, it's essential to have a complete understanding of a company's tax situation, both historically and prospectively, in order to understand how its profit margins might materially change relative to its competitors as a result of being subject to stricter accounting regulations.

As with the internal strengths and weaknesses of the SWOT analysis, many of external opportunities and threats that apply to China are common to those found in other parts of the world. These include industry trends, technology developments, government policies, and consumer tastes. The assessment of external competitive forces must include items that are unique to China. Not surprisingly, many of these external factors are driven by the Chinese government, which has its hand in almost every aspect of Chinese business.

A Chinese company needs to take into consideration whether its competitors are privately owned or state-owned. Prior to 1949, all entities in China were controlled by the government. Starting in the late 1980s, the government began to privatize many businesses, but today it still controls a substantial portion of industry at both the local, provincial, and national levels.

State-owned enterprises (SOEs) tend to be bloated organizations, because their first priority is not to maximize profits but to achieve social harmony. This is accomplished primarily by employing as many people as possible, a practice that leads to higher overhead and cost of goods. On the other hand, because SOEs are intertwined with the government, they may have access to more lucrative contracts, particularly where the customer is a branch of the government as well. From a due diligence perspective, it's important to understand what role SOEs play in the competitive landscape.

An entity's relationship with the local government, particularly on a personal level between company management and local government officials, can have a material impact on the company's business. Government policies and mandates affect all businesses in China. However, in many cases, local and provincial governments, as well as the national government, apply policies or give exemptions subjectively and unevenly. Examples would be taxation holidays, tax exemptions, relaxation of national product quality or safety standards, and exemptions from environmental regulations. Broadly speaking, these policies generally affect most participants in a given industry and will not tend to give one company a significant advantage over another. However, from a competitive standpoint, the quality of a company's relationship with government officials is always more important and can result in both industry concessions and individual favors for companies a government official may favor.

Local government officials can exert significance influence over a company's operations in many ways. First, local government officials are responsible for granting all of the applicable licenses and certificates that a company needs to operate legally in China. This includes business licenses, organization-code certificates, tax-registration certificates, production licenses for certain types of controlled products, environmental-compliance certificates, and so on. There's a healthy competition within most industries. A strong relationship with local government officials can provide a distinct advantage over competitors looking to gain access to the market.

Second, government officials can influence purchasing decisions, both within and outside of the government, steering businesses in different directions. Officials can influence where the government—and SOEs controlled by the government in a variety of industries—purchase their goods. Additionally, local businesses will often take direction from these officials as to which suppliers they should use.

Third, the local government can provide financing alternatives to bank loans or private equity. One way this occurs is through the use of government grants. The distribution of these grants is generally at the discretion of the local government, either directly or through a third party assigned by the government. Alternatively, the local government can provide low- or no-interest loans. A strong relationship with the proper officials can increase a company's chance of benefitting from these low-cost financing alternatives.

In preparing a SWOT analysis, the company should be sure to include any identifiable opportunities or threats that arise as a result of its relationship with local government officials. This may give rise to additional due diligence procedures, such as interviewing key officials, analyzing key customer relationships, or taking other steps as facts may dictate.

Chapter 9
Legal

Many of the items reviewed in full-scale legal due diligence are applicable to other areas of the due diligence process. Knowing where to find appropriate legal documentation is therefore essential—and a critical component of forensic due diligence.

Clients frequently ask us to perform cursory legal due diligence on a company. Our forensic due diligence in this area is not meant to replace the due diligence performed by a law firm. Instead, it's intended to identify existing and potential areas of legal exposure for the company, its officers, and its directors. However, out of necessity, many of the documents examined by an attorney performing legal due diligence overlap with documents examined by forensic accountants. Assets, business licenses, loan agreements, and land-ownership certificates are but four examples of this overlap.

Legal documentation in China may reside at the national, provincial, or even the local level of government. As a result, determining the location of legal documents is always a challenge in performing due diligence, as, unlike most Western countries, there's limited online remote access to this documentation. Instead, it normally takes a trip to a government agency—and the cooperation of both the company and the government official—to gain physical or onsite online access to the documents you wish to examine. In addition, depending on the document involved, even if the company is with you and authorizes the viewing of the document you request, the government official may decline to provide the document for viewing. The reason for this is that agency rules, at various levels of government, may prohibit anyone outside the agency involved from viewing the document. The Chinese mind-set on this is usually that the company or individual should already have possession of the document in question. If that's not the case, it's not up to the government to provide that document. This obviously makes it difficult to independently verify documentation.

Legal due diligence generally begins with the local Administration of Industry and Commerce (AIC). A visit to the AIC or its website will produce a great deal of legal documentation on the company, such as data regarding the company's incorporation, legal representatives, and other pertinent information.[4]

A verification of assets should also be made early in the due diligence process. An onsite inspection of manufacturing or other business facilities should correlate with the company's financials. It's also advisable to obtain an independent valuation of assets that have an impact on those financials. This is especially true with real estate.

Land Rights

As we've previously mentioned, there are two types of land-use rights in China: granted and allocated. *Granted* gives someone full ownership of the land. *Allocated*, in contrast, gives someone the right to use the land or have a long-term lease on the property. Each type of ownership will have a different inherent value. Verification of land rights can be done at the local land bureau.

One point of note is that a village collective may hold the land rights in rural areas. In this situation, it's necessary to have a signed approval from the head of the collective before a transfer of land can take place.

Employment Contracts

Employment rules in China are different from those in other parts of the world. It's therefore critical to have an understanding of how these rules work. For example, it's a requirement in China that all full-time workers have a written contract specifying the following:

- length of contract
- job description
- location of employment
- working conditions
- wages
- disciplinary actions to which the employee may be subject

An employment contract must be provided within one month of the date the employment begins.[42] If the employer fails to receive a signed contract from the employee within this thirty-day period, it must then pay double wages to the employee until a contract is signed.[43] An employer can avoid this liability for failing to conclude a written contract with a reluctant employee by terminating the employee before the thirty-day period has expired.

There are three types of Chinese employee contracts:

1. Fixed-term
2. Non–fixed term or open-ended
3. Project

While a fixed-term contract terminates on a specified date and an open-ended contract has no definitive termination date, the project contract is issued for employees who work on a specific set of tasks designated in the contract and terminates with the completion of those tasks.

An employer can establish a probationary period for an employee to determine whether the employee's skills are in line with the company's expectations. The maximum length of this probationary period varies with the length of the contract executed by the employee. For contracts of between three months and one year in length, the maximum probationary period is one month.[43] For contracts ranging between one and three years, the probationary period is two months. For a three-year or open-ended contract, it's six months.

Chinese law requires employers to inform employees of working and safety conditions before they sign an employment contract and prior to beginning a job.

According to University of Hawaii law professor Ronald Brown in his book *East Asian Labor and Employment Law,* all Chinese contracts must be in writing and should contain the following:[44]

- name, address, and legal representative of the employer
- name, address, and identification number of the employee
- duration of employment
- job description and work site
- working hours, rest periods, and vacations
- labor remuneration
- social insurance
- labor conditions, working conditions, and occupational-hazard prevention, as well as other matters stipulated by laws and regulations
- protection of confidential information, trade secrets, and intellectual property (if applicable)
- competition restrictions (limited to senior management and technical personnel).

Provisions like performance, termination, severance pay, collective contracts (for a group of employees), and dispute resolution are addressed by applicable sections of local, provincial, and national law. If an employer places competition restrictions in the contract, it is obligated to pay the former employee postemployment compensation in monthly installments. This amount usually ranges from 20 to 60 percent of an employee's monthly salary. The limit for postemployment compensation is two years.

A part-time employee is defined as anyone who works for the same employer an average of not more than four hours per day and not more than twenty-four hours in aggregate per week. If these hours are exceeded, the employee is considered to be working full-time and will then be governed by applicable regulations covering full-time employment. In the case of a part-time employee, the employer is not required to have a contract; an oral agreement will suffice. The employer may terminate part-time employees at will and without severance pay.[45] There's no probationary period for a part-time worker.

Intellectual Property

Recognizing how intellectual property in China differs from other nations is important when performing forensic due diligence on Chinese companies. There are four types of intellectual property in China:

1. Patents
2. Trademarks
3. Copyrights
4. Trade secrets

China has a first-to-file patent system in place, whereby patents are granted to those who file first, even if the person filing first was not the original inventor.[46] This is in stark contrast to the United States and the European Union, which have a first-to-invent rule.

If a patent application is made by a foreign company in China, that company must have a business address in China or utilize the services of an authorized patent agent. Patents are filed with the State Intellectual Property Office in Beijing, with administrative enforcement delegated to the provincial and municipal levels of government.

China also has a first-to-register system for trademarks that requires no evidence of prior use or ownership. Foreign parties not having a business address in China must utilize the services of an authorized trademark agent.

Copyrights differ from patents and trademarks in that they don't need to be registered between signatory countries to the Berne Convention. China and the United States are two of these signatory countries. However, registering copyrights does simplify ownership disputes.[47] If a foreign party wishes to register its copyright(s) with the China National Copyright Administration, which evidences ownership, it would then be entitled to enforcement action in China.

Regulatory Matters

Regulatory matters include any investigation, inquiry, sanctions, or other actions imposed by an overseeing government agency. This could include matters like tax audits, environmental sanctions, or inquiries from securities-regulating bodies. The company should provide all written correspondence or other documentation related to any regulatory matters. Where possible, the investigating party should also use public records to independently determine whether there are any unreported regulatory matters.

Chapter 10

Government Relationships

Government Oversight

All companies in China are directly or indirectly influenced by the Chinese government. The government may not be one of the company's board members or have an equity position in the company, but it does influence almost every aspect of a company's business. Part of this influence is a result of the Chinese State Constitution of 1982, which specifies that the government is to guide the country's economic development by making broad decisions on economic priorities and policies.[48]

Some of the things the government influences are the granting of subsidies to businesses, the issuance of licenses, and the providing of land-use certificates, permits, and other forms of approval necessary for a business to operate. In addition, the government allocates power, water, land, and other essentials for an ongoing business. Therefore, as we've previously mentioned, government relationships are extremely important in China.

If, for example, you have a good relationship with a government official and your competitor doesn't, you may get access to a new power line, which will likely be placed very close to your facility, thereby allowing you to expand your business; or a new water line that allows your business to comply with increasingly strict environmental regulations regarding treatment of a company's environmental waste; or the right to purchase land adjacent to your property, which the government would otherwise not be inclined to sell.

The government indirectly controls the allocation of contracts. It normally does this by suggesting to the company awarding the contract that it believes your company is the best suited. In China, you don't need much more justification or direction. If the government is supportive of you and your company, you'll likely prosper. If not, you'll probably be forced to merge with your competitor or suffer a rapid decline in contracts as well as a painfully slow permit process.

Government Subsidies

According to Article 1 of the prevailing Agreement on Subsidies and Countervailing Measure, applicable to all World Trade Organization (WTO) members, a subsidy exists if there is a direct or indirect financial contribution by a government, or any form of income or price support where a benefit is conferred. Based on these criteria, the Chinese government subsidizes domestic companies in the following ways:

- tax subsidies
- preferential loans
- loan guarantees
- debt forgiveness
- grants
- transfer of resources
- equity Infusions
- direct or indirect tax relief
- discount for goods and services
- exemption of import charges
- remission
- worker-related subsidies
- payment for internal transport of freight
- payment for freight charges for export shipments
- upstream subsidies

Chinese firms will sometimes receive a lower tax rate from the government relative to what they would normally pay. In addition, both national and local governments may use their influence to assist the company in obtaining a loan that exceeds the company's normal borrowing capabilities. They do this by either guaranteeing the company's loan or using their influence with the bank. In some cases, the government will arrange for forgiveness of a company's debt, or the issuance of grants to assist a company in becoming more financially viable.

The Chinese government provides subsidies for two reasons. The first is to reward a company for taking part in a government-sponsored social program, such as providing jobs in a socially disadvantaged region. The second is for enhancing China's economic well-being. Examples of this would include companies that develop an industry the government views as important, that promote technological development, or that enhance the country's economic competitiveness.

From a due diligence perspective, there are certain procedures that can and should be performed relative to subsidies. For direct financial assistance provided by the government—such as grants, direct loans, or loan guarantees—there's typically a solid paper trail documenting the transactions. These items should be reviewed in detail to understand their nature, noting features like the granting institution, the amount, the reason for the grant, the regularity of the grant, any repayment requirements, and other salient facts. Where possible, it's also advisable to directly interview the government agent responsible for implementing the grant to confirm the information in the paperwork.

Taxing and Regulatory Authority

The Ministry of Finance is in charge of setting tax policy within China, while the State Administration of Taxation (SAT) is responsible for tax collection.[49] There are twenty-five different types of taxes in China, divided into eight categories.[50] For a complete discussion of independent verification procedures related to taxation filings, please refer to chapter 11, "Independent Procedures."

Value-Added Tax

The value-added tax (VAT) is imposed on the entity and individual engaged in marketing goods—providing processing, providing repair or replacement services, or importing goods within China. The VAT taxpayer is classified as either general or a small-scale. For the general taxpayer, the VAT is imposed on the incremental value of its sale (or import) of goods or provision of processing, as well as the repair and/or replacement services. The basic tax rate is 17 percent, the lower tax rate is 13 percent, and the tax rate for export goods is 0.

For the small-scale taxpayer, a simplified system of computation of tax payable is applied, with that tax rate set at 3 percent. Generally, the prescribed time limit for paying VAT is one month. In addition, based on the amount of VAT payable by the taxpayer, there may be six other types of time limits that are applicable for paying VAT. These are one day, three days, five days, ten days, fifteen days, and one quarter. The prescribed time limit of one quarter only applies to the small-scale taxpayer. The taxpayer shall file tax returns within the period from the first day to the fifteenth day of the next month. If the tax cannot be paid within the designated time limit, the taxpayer may pay tax on each transaction.

Consumption Tax

The consumption tax is imposed on the entity and individual engaged in the producing, consigned processing, or importing of taxable consumer goods within China. The scope of the consumption tax covers fourteen taxable items, including tobacco, alcohol and alcoholic drinks, cosmetics, jewelry, and precious stones. The consumption tax payable is assessed—under the rate-on-value method or the amount on volume method—on the basis of the volume of sales or the quantity of sales, or on taxable consumer goods, respectively. The prescribed time limit for paying consumption tax is the same as that for VAT.

Business Tax

The business tax is imposed on the entity and individual engaged in providing taxable services, transferring intangible assets, or selling immovable property within China. Taxable services cover seven tax items. These include the transportation industry, the building industry, and the finance and insurance industry. The business tax payable shall be calculated on the basis of the business turnover and the amount of transfer or sales volume in respect to the taxable services or taxable activities at the statutory tax rate.

The tax rate applicable to the entertainment industry, for example, is 20 percent. However, the tax rate applicable to billiards clubs and bowling halls in this industry is 5 percent, while the tax rate applicable to all other tax items is 3 or 5 percent. The prescribed time limit for paying a business tax is the same as those for the VAT and the consumption tax.

Income Tax

There are three types of income tax:

1. Enterprise income tax
2. Income tax on enterprises with foreign investment and foreign enterprises
3. Individual income tax

Income taxes are levied on the profits realized by a producer or the income earned by an individual.

All enterprises and other income-receiving organizations, excluding sole proprietorship enterprises and partnership enterprises within China, shall be the taxpayers of the enterprise income tax. Enterprises are classified into resident enterprises and nonresident enterprises.

Resident enterprises shall pay the enterprise income tax for their income sourced within and outside of China. Nonresident enterprises shall pay the enterprise income tax as determined on the basis of whether they have organizations or establishments within China and whether their income is in fact related to such organizations or establishments. In terms of the enterprise income tax, the balance derived from the total income of an enterprise in each tax year, after deducting the tax-free income, tax-exempt income, and other deductible items, as well as any permitted carry-forward loss from previous years, shall be the taxable income. The tax rate is 25 percent.

Enterprise income tax shall be calculated on the basis of a tax year that shall commence on January 1 and end on December 31 of each calendar year. A provisional enterprise income tax shall be paid in advance on a monthly or quarterly basis, settled in full at the end of the year, and receive a refund for any overpayment or a supplement for any deficiency. This essentially means that an enterprise shall, within fifteen days after the end of each month or quarter, submit provisional enterprise income tax returns and make provisional tax payments to the taxing authority. The enterprise shall also submit an annual enterprise income tax return to the tax authority and settle the amount of tax payable or refundable within five months after the end of each year.

The individual income tax is imposed on the taxable income derived by individuals. This include eleven taxable items, such as the income from wages and salaries derived by the individuals, the income from their production, and the income derived by individual industrial or commercial households. A progressive tax rate, consisting of seven levels of from 3 to 45 percent, is applied to the income derived from wages and salaries. A progressive tax rate consisting of five levels from 5 to 35 percent is applied to the income derived from production facilities and businesses, and the income from the contracted or leased operation of an enterprise or undertaking derived by individual industrial and commercial households. It should also be noted that this tax treatment is similarly applied to the investors of sole-proprietorship enterprises and partnership enterprises. In addition, a flat tax rate of 20 percent is applied to all the other types of income.

From September 1, 2011, in terms of the income from wages and salaries, the standard monthly deduction for expenses is increased from 2,000 to 3,500 yuan. The prescribed time limit for paying individual income tax is as follows:

- Tax withheld by the withholding agent is to be paid on monthly basis.
- Tax to be paid by a self-reporting taxpayer is also to be paid on a monthly basis to the state treasury, within the first fifteen days of the following month.
- Tax to be paid on income from a production or business operation derived by individual industrial and commercial households is computed on annual basis, and the provisional income tax shall be paid in advance on a monthly basis. Refunds for any overpayment, or supplement for any deficiency, is made within three months after the end of each tax year.
- Tax to be paid on income from the contracted or leased operation of enterprises and undertakings shall be computed on an annual basis and paid to the state treasury within thirty days after the end of each tax year.
- For taxpayers who derive income from outside of China, the tax payable shall be paid to the state treasury within thirty days after the end of each tax year.
- Any taxpayers who have income over 120,000 yuan in any tax year shall personally file their tax returns with the relevant tax authorities within three months after the end of each tax year.

Resource Tax

The resource tax is imposed on entities and individuals engaged in exploiting a taxable natural resource. This taxation covers seven major categories: crude oil, natural gas, coal, other nonmetal ores, ferrous ores, nonferrous ores, and salt. The resource tax is collected under the rate-on-value method as well as the amount-on-volume method. The resource tax rate applicable to crude oil and natural gas products is between 5 and 10 percent of the sales volume. The tax amount standard varies from 0.3 yuan/ton to sixty yuan/ton, depending on the kinds and locations of the resources.

Urban and Township Land-Use Tax

The urban and township land-use tax is imposed on land in cities, county towns, administrative towns, and industrial and mining districts. The tax amount standard is determined on the basis of big cities, medium-sized cities, small cities, county towns, administrative towns, and industrial and mining districts. The tax ranges from 0.6 to 30 yuan/m2.

The urban and township land-use tax is calculated on a yearly basis and is paid in installments. The prescribed time limit for paying this tax is determined by the provincial government, autonomous regions, and municipalities directly under the central government.

Special-Purpose Tax

Special-purpose taxes are taxes on specific items for which the government has designated a special regulative purpose.

City Maintenance and Construction Tax

A city maintenance and construction tax is imposed on the entities and individuals who pay value-added tax, consumption tax, and business tax. This tax is calculated on the basis of those taxes actually paid by the taxpayer. There are three levels of tax rates applied on the basis of a taxpayer's location—for example, 7 percent for an urban area, 5 percent for towns, and 1 percent for other areas. The city maintenance and construction tax shall be paid with the value-added tax, consumption tax, and business tax.

Farmland Occupation Tax

The tax on the use of arable land is imposed on the entities and individuals who use the arable land to build houses or for other nonagricultural construction purposes. This tax is collected on the basis of the area of the arable land used. The tax amount standard ranges from five to fifty yuan/m2. The taxpayer shall pay this tax on the use of arable land within thirty days upon the approval by the land administration department on the use of land.

Land Appreciation Tax

The land appreciation tax is imposed on the incremental value of the transfer of state-owned land-use rights and above-ground structures (with their attached facilities) at the specified tax rate. There are four levels of progressive tax rates: 30, 40, 50, and 60 percent.

Taxpayers shall file their tax returns with the tax authority where the real estate is located within seven days of the execution of the real estate transfer contract. They'll also pay the land appreciation tax within the time limit designated by the applicable tax authority. Where the land appreciation tax is able to be calculated, the provisional land appreciation tax may be collected in advance, settled after the completion of the project, refunded for any overpayment, or supplemented for any deficiency.

House Property Tax

The house property tax is imposed on houses within cities, county towns, administrative towns, and industrial and mining districts. The tax is calculated on the basis of the residual value or rental income of the house property. Taxpayers include house property owners, the managing entity of the house, custodians, and users. This tax rate has two categories: one in which the tax amount payable is calculated on the basis of the residual value of the house property and the applicable tax rate is 1.2 percent, and one in which the tax amount payable is calculated on the basis of the rental income of the house property and the applicable tax rate is 12 percent. However, where individuals lease their residential houses at the market price, the applicable rate is 4 percent.

House property tax is collected on a yearly basis and paid in installments. As of January 1, 2009, foreign-invested enterprises, foreign enterprises and organizations, and foreign individuals (including enterprises and organizations funded by Hong Kong, Macau and Taiwan and the compatriots of these three) shall pay the house property tax in accordance with the Provisional Regulations on House Property Tax of the People's Republic of China.

Vehicle Purchase Tax

The vehicle purchase tax is imposed on entities and individuals who purchase taxable vehicles, such as cars, motorcycles, trams, trailers, and agricultural transport vehicles. The tax is calculated under the rate-on-value method, and the tax rate is 10 percent. The price for the tax assessment is the total amount of the purchase price, along with related charges, in addition to the price paid by the taxpayer to the seller for the purpose of purchasing the taxable vehicle. This excludes value-added tax.

The SAT will provide the minimum price for the tax assessment of taxable vehicles by reference to the average market transaction price. When taxpayers purchase a taxable vehicle, they shall file their tax returns and pay the tax due in a lump sum within sixty days of the purchase.

Vehicle and Vessel Tax

The vehicle and vessel tax is imposed on vehicles and vessels within China. These must be registered with the appropriate regulatory department in accordance with the law, and the appropriate tax shall be paid by the owners or managers of the vehicles and vessels. There are six major tax categories for vehicles and vessels, including passenger vehicles and commercial vehicles. The annual tax can vary from 36 to 5,400 yuan/vehicle, from three to sixty yuan/ton in terms of deadweight (net tonnage), or from 600 to 2,000 yuan/m in terms of the length of the body of a yacht. The vehicle and vessel tax shall be filed and paid on a yearly basis.

Stamp Tax

The stamp tax is imposed on entities and individuals executing or accepting taxable instruments, as specified in tax laws during economic activities and exchanges. This tax is calculated at different proportionate tax rates in relation to the contract price or on the basis of a fixed amount per instrument. There are four levels of proportionate tax rates: 1, 0.5, 0.3, and 0.05 percent.

As an example, for a purchase and sale contract, the proportionate tax rate is 0.3 percent of the value of the purchase and sale. For a processing contract, the proportionate tax rate would be 0.5 percent of the processing fee of the contracted receipts. In terms of a property or leasing contract, it would be 1 percent of the lease amount. And for loan contracts, it would be 0.05 percent of the loan amount. For a license or permit, a fixed amount of 5 yuan shall be paid for each instrument.

To pay the stamp tax, taxpayers shall purchase and affix at one time the full corresponding amount of tax stamps. For an equity transfer instrument, the stamp tax shall be paid by the parties to such instrument at the rate of 3 percent and on the basis of the actual transaction price on the securities market upon the date of execution of such instrument.

Deed Tax

The deed tax is imposed on land and houses, the titles to which are conveyed through such means as transfer, assignment, purchase or sale, and gift or exchange. This tax shall be paid by the entities and individuals who are the transferees. Where the land or houses are the subject of a transfer, assignment, purchase, or sale, the tax shall be calculated on the basis of the transaction price. Where the land or house is given as a gift, the tax shall be assessed by the collection authority. Where the land or house is transferred through an exchange, the tax shall be calculated on the basis of the difference between the exchange prices. The tax rate will vary from 3 to 5 percent. The taxpayer shall file the tax return within ten days after the occurrence of the tax-payment obligation and pay the tax within the time limit specified by the deed tax collection authority.

Agriculture Taxes

Agriculture tax, agriculture specialty tax, animal husbandry tax, and customs duties are imposed on both the goods imported into the country, and those exported from the People's Republic of China.

Environmental

In recent years, the local, provincial, and national governments within China have become more serious about protecting the environment. This hasn't always been the case. For the past three decades, in order to fuel the country's meteoric growth, all levels of government ignored the environment, as well as environmental laws, in order to encourage the expansion of their manufacturing and energy base. Recently, however, there's been a trend toward environmental sensitivity, observing environmental laws, and remediation of contaminated sites.

This is not universally the case throughout China. Local governments, in particular, are frequently not on board with preserving the environment.

Many want to create jobs—and increase their tax revenue—at any cost. As a result, forensic due diligence on the environmental aspects of a company's operations is critically important, as China's environmental issues have been ignored for so long that many companies have enormous problems in this area.

When evaluating potential environmental issues, it's important to do the following:[51]

- Obtain copies of the company's environmental permits, licenses, and authorizations.
- Obtain a copy of the company's environmental policies.
- Evaluate the company's environmental record-keeping, especially in regard to internal reporting procedures, monitoring reports, and internal/external audits.
- Review the company's records for communication with environmental regulatory agencies, especially in regard to violation notices, consent decrees, administrative orders, and environmental litigation matters.
- Obtain a copy of property surveys, plats, and drawings noting the locations of wetlands, bodies of water, storm-water easements, detention-pond agreements, flood-zone designations, endangered species habitats, and historical sites.
- Determine if any entity outside the company has mineral, timber, or other natural resource rights on the company's owned or leased land.
- Determine if the manner in which adjacent land is utilized could contribute to pollution on the company's property.
- Obtain from the company a listing of all hazardous substances used.
- Obtain from the company a description of on- and off-site waste-disposal practices.
- Obtain the locations of underground storage tanks, as applicable.
- Interview the company's owners and workers, as well as surrounding businesses and residents, for past or present environmental issues.

- Perform an exterior and interior analysis of the company's properties, both owned and leased, for any outward signs of environmental issues.
- Obtain a copy of any environmental insurance policies.
- Determine the company's current and anticipated expenditures for environmental compliance and remediation, as required.
- Take a physical soil and groundwater sampling from various parts of the company's property, both owned and leased, and send these samples in for laboratory analysis.

Chapter 11

Independent Procedures

Independent verification procedures are often the most critical part of a Chinese due diligence. To this point, we've focused on describing procedures for gathering, examining, and evaluating evidence related to the entity's corporate structure, finances, and operations. This type of work is the foundation for a wide variety of due diligence assignments, whether it be for a potential merger or acquisition, financing, public listing, joint venture, shareholder investigation, or other type of transaction.

A large portion of a typical Chinese due diligence file is comprised of documents like capital verification reports; business licenses; financial reports; vendor and customer contracts; bank statements; and other documents that the company maintains in its files. These records are used as evidence to attempt to verify critical facts about the company—for example, that the company was duly organized; that it operates legally and within the scope provided by the government of the People's Republic of China (PRC); that its financial information is reasonably accurate; that its customers and vendors are real; and that its cash balances are legitimate.

While collection and review of documents provided by the company is a necessary and integral part of the Chinese forensic due diligence process, it's not nearly enough on its own to provide substantial comfort in most due diligence projects. The reason is very simple: accounting documents, contracts, customers, suppliers, and all types of transactions can be falsified by a company in order to perpetrate a fraud. Examining documents and evaluating their legitimacy provides a baseline level of comfort. However, independent corroboration of critical facts by parties that do not have a vested interest in the performance of the company provides a substantially better body of evidence when reaching a conclusion on a due diligence assignment.

Each situation that requires due diligence has its own unique characteristics. Based on our experience in China, however, there are a handful of critical independent procedures that we end up performing over and over again. Our goal is to verify critical business transactions, especially in areas where fraud is common, with external parties who are not stakeholders in the business. We design these procedures to create as many objective cross-references as possible and to provide a degree of comfort regarding the accuracy of the company's financial results and other business representations.

Tax Verification and Reconciliation

Perhaps the most common issue that arises for Chinese companies that perform a transaction that requires any sort of due diligence is an inability to reconcile tax reports filed with the PRC government to reported financial statements. This can have disastrous consequences on many fronts, ranging from damage inflicted by short sellers to regulatory issues with the US Securities and Exchange Commission (SEC) to statutory issues with the Chinese government.

The term "reported financial statement" primarily refers to any type of report of financial results or position reported to, or filed with, an external party. This includes lending banks, potential equity or debt investors, securities regulatory bodies, or prospective acquirers. Many privately held Chinese companies looking to complete a fundraising, public listing, or acquisition transaction run into a common problem:

they maintain at least two sets of books. One is used for external reporting and the other is used for tax reporting.

The external books generally include all company transactions in an effort to report the highest possible sales, income, or cash flow figures. This is done to maximize valuation or borrowing ability and generally makes the company appear as financially successful as possible. The tax books have a completely different purpose: to reduce the amount of corporate income tax paid. These records generally reflect much lower sales and income numbers, which results in a lower income tax liability.

The most common situation we encounter is that even when the external books show substantial sales and income, the tax books reflect only modest sales and a very small amount of income on which the company pays corporate income tax. Under-reporting sales and income to the taxing authorities is a common practice and is generally condoned, either implicitly or explicitly, by the local taxing authority.

Corporate income tax is instituted at the federal level by the State Administration for Taxation (SAT). It's either collected by local branch offices of the SAT or paid through the SAT's online system. Historically, it's been a common but unofficial practice for the local SAT offices to set a quota for a company. This quota establishes the income tax a company should expect to pay within a specified period of time. Management can then tailor the company's tax records to reflect an appropriate amount of sales that, after applying a reasonable cost of goods sold and overhead costs, results in an income that coincidentally generates an income tax liability approximately equal to the quota.

There's a second purpose for multiple books, and that's to manipulate the amount of value-added tax (VAT) paid. As previously mentioned, value-added tax is a form of consumption tax whereby the seller in a transaction is taxed only on the value added to a product by the stage of manufacture or distribution completed by the seller. The seller collects the gross amount of the VAT payable to the government, which is calculated as a percentage of the sale price, from its customer. The seller then deducts the VAT payments made on purchases from its own suppliers related to the manufacture or distribution of the product.

This results in the seller paying a net tax on the increase in the sales price, from the input materials it purchased to the final product it sold. This is equivalent to the "value added" by the seller. VAT regulations are also governed by the SAT. Current VAT rates are either 13 or 17 percent of the sales price invoiced, depending on the product and the industry.

VAT, like corporate income tax, is self-reported. In China, this means that companies take advantage of the situation. As previously mentioned, the reporting process for VAT is that a formal government invoice, called a *fapiao* (发票), is issued by the seller for each and every transaction. The buyer uses the fapiao as documentation for the input deduction. When buyers process or distribute the product and resell it, they in turn issue a fapiao to the new purchaser of the product and likewise use the self-issued fapiao as evidence of the sale for VAT reporting purposes. This system works well if all parties in the chain issue a fapiao and report all transactions on their VAT returns. However, this is not what happens in practice.

The most common form of VAT avoidance is for sellers to collude with their customers and reach an agreement that no fapiao will be issued for a particular transaction. This would seem to benefit only the seller, who has presumably received a fapiao and paid VAT for input costs and, therefore, will not report the sale and pay the related VAT thereon.

On the surface, it's difficult to see what's in it for buyers, since they can't deduct input costs because they don't receive a fapiao from the seller. It would seem that they're left on the hook for the entire VAT bill in the absence of deductions. In reality, however, the most common practice is that the seller will offer the product at a discount that's large enough to compensate the buyer for the risk of being unable to offset the lost deduction—but that's still smaller than the applicable VAT rate. The buyer will then make an agreement with the next buyer so that no fapiao will be issued for the next transaction in the chain, which will also be done at a discount. The buyer will then report no deductions for the purchase and will also report no VAT liability on the sale of the product, while still making the sale at a reasonable "true" profit. Fapiao non-issuance generally continues to the end of the chain, such that the end user of the product does not pay VAT on the final purchase, since the last seller in the chain will not have a fapiao on inputs to deduct.

The seller in the middle of the chain ends up making approximately the same gross profit on goods sold with or without a fapiao. The question one may ask is, why risk disregarding tax laws? The primary reason is that there are customers who will only purchase goods for which a fapiao is not issued. As a result, sellers who insist on issuing a fapiao will miss out on this incremental revenue and profit, as buyers will take their business elsewhere. Additionally, fraudulent fapiao's are very easy to purchase in China, so companies can simply buy blank invoices and create their own deductions.

The accounting for the manufacturing and distribution process is obviously more complicated than the simplified example shown above. Non-fapiao transactions are generally done on a case-by-case basis, with the decision maker keeping a close watch on the financial results and tax situation—and making adjustments accordingly in order to meet the desired tax target.

For privately held Chinese companies, these types of tax strategies are commonplace, with one universal goal: to increase cash flow to the company and, ultimately, to the principal equity holders by lowering their tax payments. That works just fine as long as the company remains a closely held private enterprise operating in China. But what happens when it ventures outside of the PRC and becomes subject to the rules propagated by other regulatory bodies?

Between 2006 and 2010, a total of 339 Chinese companies listed on the major US stock markets—106 on New York Stock Exchange (NYSE) and 233 on NASDAQ. Cases of fraud and resulting shareholder lawsuits were widespread, with forty-one class-action lawsuits filed against US-listed Chinese companies through November 2011.[52]

Many of the fraud cases have been brought to light by short sellers, who look to profit from the declining price of a stock. In a self-fulfilling prophecy, a stock's decline in value is often caused by expository reports published by the short sellers themselves. These reports cause distrust with investors, who then sell the stock of the company and drive down the stock price.

Short sellers will go to great lengths to point out any and all informational misrepresentations, characterizing these as fraud on the part of the company meant to swindle investors. One of the first places they start in their examination of a company is with tax reporting. They look at the revenue, income, and balance sheet information that a company has filed with the PRC taxing authorities. They then compare these figures with the same publicly available information published with the SEC. This information will almost never agree on first blush, and there the short sellers have their first piece of ammunition.

The most common approach taken by short sellers is to compare SEC financial information to two tax reports: federal income tax returns filed with the SAT and financial reports filed with the State Administration for Industry and Commerce (SAIC). The SAIC is the Chinese government agency responsible for issuing and renewing companies' business licenses. The SAIC acts like the individual secretary of state offices in the United States, and its primary responsibility is overseeing corporate registrations of all companies in China through thousands of local branch offices throughout the country. All companies in China are required to file annual PRC GAAP–audited financial results with the SAIC. Also, each separate legal entity in a consolidated group of companies must file an annual report with the SAIC.

Although short sellers make claims of fraud, it's actually very difficult for an outside party—meaning someone without the company's consent—to access restricted tax and SAIC filings and make a meaningful comparison between a company's published financial statements and financial information provided to the PRC government. There are several reasons for this:

1. Tax reports filed with the SAIC and SAT are not publicly available, so any party who claims to have independently obtained copies of such tax reports without the consent of the company more than likely bribed an employee to get the information.
2. There are legitimate reconciling items between tax and external reporting accounting. If a company is listed in the US, its financial statements must be prepared in accordance with US GAAP (generally accepted accounting principles). There are a substantial number of differences in accounting conventions between US GAAP and locally used PRC GAAP, as well as accounting ramifications at the parent level that would not be reflected in tax reports. In fact, many US-listed Chinese companies prominently disclose a footnote in their "Critical Accounting Policies" that explains this. Accordingly, there are any number of accounting entries that could be made pursuant to US GAAP that would not be made under PRC GAAP. Common examples of reconciling items include derivative accounting related to financing transactions at the parent level; stock based compensation expenses at the parent level; cutoff of sales or purchases between periods; and intercompany transactions between entities of the same consolidated group, all of which must file separate SAT and SAIC reports but report to the SEC on a consolidated basis.
3. Reporting companies that have multiple operating subsidiaries report their results to the SEC on a consolidated basis, with some financial information disclosed by segment. For tax purposes, however, each legal entity in the PRC reports to the government

individually. It would be near impossible for someone without access to the company's consolidation workings to reconcile tax reports on an entity-by-entity basis. While they could compare the consolidated sales and income and note whether those amounts reconciled, it would be difficult to pinpoint the source of the problem without access to nonpublic records.

Despite the difficulty that third parties encounter in trying to independently prove tax fraud, the mere suggestion of fraudulent practice can be enough to send a stock plummeting. As a result, many listed Chinese companies have engaged independent due diligence practitioners to verify that their tax declarations are in compliance with Chinese tax law in order to offset the accusations made by short sellers. A company-engaged due diligence team is able to directly verify tax reports and payments and reconcile to reported financial results, since the company assists the due diligence team in obtaining documents directly from the taxing authorities and banks.

Our general process for reconciling a Chinese company's tax filings to the audited financial information reported in its public filings is as follows:

1. Obtain and review management account financial data. This is raw financial data in the form of general ledger outputs or trial balances extracted from the company's general ledger system.
2. Independently obtain reports filed with the SAIC by visiting the local SAIC office, observing the filing in the computer system, and observing a copy of the report(s) being printed by the tax official. We view the filing in the SAIC's system by looking at the screen of the government employee assisting us. This is to ensure that the employee was not simply handed a photocopy of a fraudulent SAIC report by the company prior to our arrival and is then, in turn, providing the report to us. By reviewing the screen, we confirm that the financial results included in the printed report are, in fact, what exists in the SAIC's system.

3. Independently verify amounts filed with the SAT. This task is more problematic than verifying the SAIC reports themselves since it is not SAT policy to provide copies of previously filed reports, even to the company themselves. Therefore, visiting the SAT office and obtaining a hard copy of the report is almost never an option.

   Companies can file income taxes either online, using the SAT's secure database, or in person at the tax office. If the company files its income tax returns online, we log in to its database using the company's access codes, which the company provides for us, and then review and print filed data directly from the government website. This is the most ideal situation, as the government database is easily recognizable and would, as a result, be very difficult to forge on a standalone company basis.

   For manual SAT filers, we cannot obtain direct independent confirmation that returns provided by the company were, in fact, filed with the SAT. Instead, we cross-reference the following:

   a. all financial information in company-provided SAT tax return to the independently obtained SAIC report
   b. sales on the SAT tax return to stamped and filed VAT returns provided by the company
   c. sales on the SAT tax return to sales in the online government VAT filing system (see step 4 below) using the company's login information, if the company is an online VAT filer.

   We also examine the original SAT tax return provided by the company, which reflect the government chop, and analyze it for authenticity.

4. Independently verify sales reported on VAT returns. The most objective evidence comes from logging on to the online VAT reporting system using the company's access codes and then verifying filed data. However, historical VAT data is not available for more than a few months, so we must accept stamped copies provided by the company if the time frame we're reviewing is

more than a few months old. We then rely on cross-referencing this to SAIC reports and VAT returns. We also examine the hard-copy forms and then analyze the forms and chops for authenticity.

5. Reconcile the balance sheet and income statement published in SAIC reports, SAT returns, and VAT returns to management accounts for each subsidiary. There are often reconciling items between the management accounts and the various tax forms. In some cases, these are legitimate reconciling items, such as government grants that are nontaxable and therefore not reflected in SAT returns, but which are reflected in management accounts.

   There are also reconciling items that, while not technically legitimate differences between tax and book reporting, are common practice in China. A good example of this type of difference is revenue for items shipped at the end of the fiscal year which are properly recognized as book income, but then are incorrectly left out of tax income until the following year. While the revenue technically should be recognized for tax purposes when it's shipped, in practice it's only reported to the government when a fapiao is issued. Many Chinese companies will complete a sale but then wait until a later time, sometimes the following fiscal year, to issue the invoice in order to defer the tax liability to the following period. We explain each of these differences in our reconciliation in a tabular format.

6. Obtain consolidation worksheets from the audit file that shows the combination of the management accounts of all subsidiaries, US GAAP eliminations, US GAAP adjusting journal entries, and the conversion from local currency to US dollars. We then reconcile the US dollar combined and adjusted financials to the financial statements published in the company's SEC filings. This ensures that the subsidiary-level financial information that we tested to tax reports does in fact comprise the results reported to the investing public.

7. Finally, we verify all tax payments shown on the VAT and SAT declaration forms by reconciling payments to independently obtained bank statements. We go to the bank(s) where the company's tax accounts are held. With the company's authorization, we have bank personnel print bank statements from their system for applicable periods. This is another procedure that outside parties cannot perform without the assistance of the company.

After performing the above procedures, we prepare a report detailing the findings and explaining all reconciling items. We then offer our conclusions on the likelihood that tax reports agree to reported financial information, based on the strength and independence of the evidence that we reviewed.

The most common criticism of this approach is that, since we're engaged and paid by the company, we're not truly independent, and therefore, our conclusions are not worth much. However, as we've described, certain information that's critical to reaching a viable conclusion on the validity of financial information and tax reports simply cannot be obtained without the company's assistance. This includes items like copies of tax returns, access to the SAT and VAT filing databases, bank statements, and detailed consolidation information. Without this information, conclusions drawn by short sellers and other independent researchers are incomplete, uninformed, and—in our experience—often inaccurate.

The process we employ is similar to that of public accounting firms performing a financial audit, in that we take information provided by the company and use our knowledge of business and institutional processes in the company's business environment to independently verify that information in the most thorough and reliable manner possible. For informed investors simply looking for objective information, that's a very valuable service. From the company's perspective, full transparency regarding tax and financial compliance is a precious asset when your peer group is assumed to always be breaking the rules.

Because of the nature of China's tax reporting system, it's impossible to achieve unquestioned reliability on the company's tax representations. However, we believe these procedures provide the best framework to determine their validity.

Cash Verification

Another common, and recently high-profile, form of financial fraud perpetrated by Chinese companies is cash fraud. In its most common form, cash fraud is the overstatement of the amount of cash held at a given time on the company's balance sheet. This has the obvious effect of falsely inflating the company's working capital and net assets in general and its financial health overall. But cash fraud is not limited to the balance sheet alone. It's usually a consequence of previously undetected revenue fraud.

When a company overstates revenue—and consequently income—by reporting sales that did not actually occur, the trouble it runs into is where to book the offsetting accounting entry. In a real sales transaction, the offset to revenue is either in accounts receivable, if sold with credit terms, or in cash, if paid at the time of sale. In the case of products sold on credit, the account receivable is eventually paid by the customer and thus converted to cash. When making fraudulent sales, companies will often "sell" the product to a fictitious corporation established for the purpose of receiving the sale, to a real corporation under common control with company ownership, or to a friendly third party who agrees to "buy" the products with the implicit understanding that they'll be returned to the company at a later date with no cash actually changing hands.

However, when a company is audited, the auditors are very careful to review the collectability of accounts receivable—which means that "old" sales that have not been collected within a reasonable period of time must be written down. This results in a bad debt charge to income that offsets the revenue previously recognized, though not always in the same accounting period. In order to avoid taking this write-down, more sophisticated perpetrators of this type of fraud will transfer this balance out of accounts receivable after a reasonable period of time, before it's noticed by the auditors and has to be written down. But where do they transfer the balance?

Some Chinese companies hide it in plain sight in the cash balance. From a bookkeeping perspective, they show cash being received and relieving the outstanding sales account receivable. This type of fraud would be very difficult to pull off in the US or another jurisdiction where banking regulations and reporting are much more sophisticated than in China. Auditors in the US can very easily uncover this type of scheme through bank confirmations.

One of the most basic procedures in an audit is for the auditors to directly mail bank confirmations to the banking institution to confirm bank balances and activity. The auditors mail a confirmation form to the bank, with the client's authorization, and a bank official completes the form with the company's account balances as of the audit date, along with other information. The form is then mailed directly from the bank to the auditors to prevent tampering by the company. These forms are very common and mostly standardized in the Western world. Banking institutions recognize these forms and complete them as a matter of course. There are also significant deterrents against falsifying these confirmations, including criminal penalties for both the company and the bank representatives for perpetrating this type of fraud.

Accordingly, auditors rely heavily on these bank confirmations as a key piece of audit evidence, and they can place a substantial amount of reliance that the confirmation was completed in good faith by the banking representatives. However, this "mail and return" bank confirmation policy does not work as well in parts of the world where corruption and collusion are routine business practices—and where operators are beyond the reach of US regulatory bodies.

One of the more egregious examples of fraudulent accounting practices by a Chinese company is Longtop Financial Technologies Ltd. (Longtop), a China-based software company that traded on the New York Stock Exchange. Longtop had a market capitalization of over a billion dollars—until their auditors sent them a very dramatic resignation letter detailing large-scale cash fraud. In a letter from Deloitte Touche Tohmatsu CPA Ltd. (Deloitte) to Longtop's audit committee, dated May 17, 2011, as published in Longtop's Form 6-K filed with the SEC on May 23, 2011, Deloitte outlined that, in the process of performing follow-up bank confirmation procedures in person at Longtop's banks, they made several disturbing discoveries. These included statements by bank staff that their bank had no record of certain transactions.

Confirmation replies previously received by Deloitte were said to be false. There were significant differences in deposit balances reported by the bank staff and the amounts identified in confirmations previously received by Deloitte and compared to Longtop's books and records. There were significant bank borrowings reported by bank staff that were not in bank confirmations previously received by Deloitte and were also not recorded in Longtop's books and records. When Deloitte auditors then attempted to initiate additional bank confirmation procedures as a result of these findings, they were informed that Longtop made calls to the banks asserting that Deloitte was not its auditor and secured the company's second-round bank confirmation documentation that was located on the bank premises.

Threats were made by the company to stop Deloitte's staff from leaving company premises unless they left audit files behind. The company's staff also took certain Deloitte working papers. Deloitte further claimed that Longtop's chairman of the board later called a Deloitte partner and informed him, in the course of the conversation, that "there were fake revenue in the past so there were fake cash recorded on the books."

Deloitte had previously issued six clean audit opinions for Longtop. Based on the publicly disclosed letter from Deloitte, the auditors had been relying on mailed confirmations to the bank until their suspicions led them to perform in-person bank verification procedures.

In China, it's relatively easy for company managers who want to carry out this type of fraud to get around the traditional US-style mailed bank confirmation. There's usually a personal relationship between a principal of the company, most likely the chairman or another significant shareholder, and one or more high-ranking bank employees. Because local branch banks have a high degree of autonomy from the central banking infrastructure, they're run more like community banks. Companies that are large or important enough to be blessed by the local or provincial government for a foreign listing tend to have clout with local banks, as they normally provide the banks with a substantial amount of business. Accordingly, bank and company executives are likely to have a close business and personal relationship.

This is especially true in rural areas where it would not be uncommon for a company chairman to ask a bank executive to disregard an auditor confirmation request, or even mail or fax an already completed version supplied by the company, to the auditors. Even where bank executives are not willing to be directly complicit in falsifying the confirmation, a phone call from the chairman telling the bank executive to disregard the incoming confirmation request, since the auditors are no longer engaged by the company, would likely result in no confirmation response from the bank. This opens the door for the company to falsify one of its own.

As many of these types of fraud have been brought to light—and many others are never made public when companies can't pass an initial audit and subsequently can't achieve a public listing—auditors have taken to refining their cash auditing procedures for Chinese companies. The most common method they now employ is onsite bank confirmation, where the auditors send staff directly to the bank to confirm balances. Additionally, as online banking access becomes more common in

China, auditors often log on to the company's internet banking site and review bank data directly.

In many cases, we're brought in to review bank confirmation procedures performed by auditors and to verify that the reported cash balances are accurate. We generally verify cash balances as of a recent quarterly or annual reporting date. Our goal is to validate all, or substantially all, of the cash balances reported in the company's publicly filed financial statements. Our procedures for verifying cash balances generally follow the pattern outlined below:

1. We have the company prepare a schedule of all cash accounts that are included in the consolidated reported cash balance, including the bank name and location, account number, account type, balance as of the verification date, and currency denomination.
2. We reconcile the cash balances on the schedule into the company's general ledger system to ensure that the balances reconcile to the reporting system.
3. We go to each bank located in China to verify the cash balances in person. Our goal at each bank is to meet with a bank official and view the account activity and ending balances for each account on the computer screen at the bank to confirm that the balances are indeed being sourced from the bank's computer system. We then have the bank print statements for us as far back as they're willing and able. Our experience has been that, at most, banks in China are able to maintain approximately six months' worth of detailed activity and balances in the accessible portion of their system before that data is archived. Once archived, bank data must be accessed through an application made to the central branch of the applicable bank.
4. We make sure that the printed statements from the bank reconcile to the information we view on the bank's computer screen.

5. We reconcile the activity and ending balances on the bank statements to the activity and balances in the company's general ledger. We check the bank statements for any unusually large cash transactions, in or out. We also check for any cash transactions that exist in either the general ledger or the bank statements, but not in both, which could indicate cash manipulation.
6. Generally, for Chinese companies listed on a foreign exchange, substantially all of their cash balances are located in Chinese banks. Even with corporate structures that can include multiple offshore holding companies, cash is usually held in China because of the cost and difficulty of moving it offshore as a result of Chinese government currency controls. These offshore corporations are commonly held in Hong Kong, the British Virgin Islands, and the US. In many cases, we can log in to the company's online banking system directly and download statements for these accounts. Alternatively, if required, we will perform direct confirmation procedures applicable to the jurisdiction of the bank, usually in the form of a mailed confirmation.
7. We have the company provide us with a consolidation worksheet that shows the combination of management accounts from all subsidiaries; US GAAP eliminations and adjusting journal entries; and any conversions from local currency to US dollars. We then reconcile the subsidiary-level cash balances to the amounts tested, and the resulting US dollar combined and adjusted financials to the financial statements published in the company's SEC filings. This ensures that subsidiary-level cash activity and balances that we compared to bank statements is the same data used in the company's published financial statements.

Using these procedures, we're usually able to verify more than 95 percent of reported cash balances to statements obtained either directly from the bank or from a reliable online banking system. In some cases, we may uncover and report cash inconsistencies, reporting errors, or even fraud if the bank statements do not reconcile to the company's records. This type of testing is very useful not only in confirming the cash balance shown on the balance sheet but also in providing additional comfort that the company's reported revenue and income are less likely to be overstated. This type of fraud is more difficult to hide when cash is verified using these cash verification procedures.

Fixed-Asset Verification

Fixed assets are another area of the Chinese financial statement that can be rife with potential problems, often covering fraud in other areas of the business. We perform verification procedures on fixed assets like buildings, production equipment, vehicles, office equipment, and construction in progress. In addition, we'll confirm the company's land-use rights. These accounts can be hiding spots for fraudulent revenue.

Companies perpetrating a fraud have to do something with the fake cash they purportedly collected from a bogus sale. In our experience, companies may record the purchase of fixed assets that they did not actually buy, inflate the price of assets that were actually purchased, or "borrow" and use assets that belong to another person or entity and claim that they were purchased and are now owned outright by the company.

To provide some assurance that fixed assets the company claims in its reported financial statements are actually in use and owned by the company, we employ the following procedures:

1. We have the company provide a list of all fixed assets, including:
    a. a description of the asset,
    b. the original purchase date,
    c. the original cost,
    d. an estimated residual value applied for accounting purposes,
    e. an estimated useful life of the asset,

f. the depreciation methodology used, and
g. the amount of accumulated depreciation as of the most recent balance sheet date(s) or applicable balance sheet date(s) being tested.

2. Prior to our arrival, we have company personnel physically tag each asset listed on the schedule with a description of the asset so that it's easily matched to the schedule.
3. We make test selections from the schedule based on the scope of the assignment. In some cases, we may test every asset on the schedule. In other cases, where the assets are too numerous to count, we may seek a certain level of coverage of the total value of fixed assets that gives us comfort that the fixed-asset balance is accurately stated and there's no nonexistent or grossly overvalued assets included.
4. Once we've selected our samples, our first test is to physically view the assets. We locate the asset based on the tagging system and compare the information on the tag to that on the schedule of fixed assets to make sure it matches. We then look at the function of the asset and determine if it reasonably appears to be what the schedule purports it to be and that it's located in an appropriate position in the company's facilities that would allow it to perform its claimed function. Finally, we examine the working condition of the asset and make sure it looks reasonably new or worn compared to the age shown on the schedule.
5. Once we've confirmed that the assets exist, we reconcile each to appropriate purchasing documentation. For assets like vehicles, office equipment, and stand-alone production equipment, this usually means reconciling to a vendor contract and/or invoice. Since these documents are provided by the company, their corroboration value is relatively weak. As a result, we may also choose, on a sample basis, to personally visit the supplier and conduct an interview regarding the sale of the equipment, verifying that it was indeed sold to the company, the date it was sold, and the sale price.

6. For buildings that are part of a construction project—for example, an integrated production facility or headquarters building—we obtain a copy of the construction contract from the company and reconcile the relevant terms. This reconciliation includes items like location, land size, building size, and building description as compared to the actual building. We then reconcile the cost, per the contract, to the fixed-assets schedule. If the building is still under construction, we review the cost that's been recorded to "construction in progress" and then test the methodology for reasonableness. If the asset is complete and has been placed into service, we'll review a copy of the construction completion report issued by the construction company when the asset was finished. Since buildings often comprise a substantial portion of fixed assets, we usually meet independently with the construction company to confirm the details of the construction contract.
7. We reconcile the purchase of each tested fixed asset to supporting payment documentation, such as outgoing wire advices. We then trace payments for fixed-asset purchases to bank statements. We always recommend that the company grant us access to its banks so that we can obtain statements directly from the bank and trace payments to verified bank data. This provides us with the strongest evidence of payment authenticity. If we're not granted access, we simply reconcile to statements provided by the company and qualify in our report that the statements were not independently verified and do not provide the same level of assurance that we would receive from statements we obtained directly from the bank.
8. If possible, we obtain the company's SAIC report for the balance sheet date in question. We recommend that our staff obtain the report directly from the SAIC office to substantiate its authenticity. We then reconcile the fixed assets to the balance sheet included in the SAIC report.
9. In some cases, assets will have other third-party documentation to which we can reconcile the cost, acquisition date, or other

data. For example, companies may have appraisal reports on certain fixed assets that they used to obtain a bank loan. We inquire with management if any other documentation exists and, if it does, we evaluate this documentation on a case-by-case basis.

10. Finally, for reporting companies, we have the company provide us with its consolidation worksheet for the balance sheet date(s) under review. We then reconcile the subsidiary-level fixed-asset balances to the amounts tested, and the resulting US dollar combined and adjusted financials to financial statements published in the company's SEC filings. This ensures that the subsidiary-level fixed-asset balances we tested are the same used in the company's published financial statements.

We should note that these steps are reflective of an ideal testing scenario. In reality, each situation is different, and the scope of our work can be limited by many different factors, including the company budget for the engagement, the availability of any of the documentation described, and other mitigating factors. Because we're usually hired directly by the company, its board of directors, or a related committee of the board, we can only access the documentation they allow us to view. We always explain that in order to provide the strongest conclusion possible, we should perform all of the procedures outlined above. However, in many cases, some of these steps are eliminated, and we may be required to qualify our conclusions.

With respect to land-use rights, we employ similar but slightly different procedures. This is because land-use rights are granted directly by the government and are not sold through private suppliers. Regarding land-use rights, we employ the following procedures:

1. We have the company provide a schedule of land-use rights, including a description of the land, the date it was acquired, the amount paid, the terms of the land-use rights, and accumulated

amortization as of the most recent balance sheet date(s) or applicable balance sheet date(s) being tested.

2. We reconcile the land-use rights from the schedule to land-use rights agreements with the government entity that granted the rights.
3. If possible, we visit the site of the land to make sure the description matches that in the contract.
4. We examine the original land-use certificate issued by the government for each property. We examine the certificate(s) for authenticity as well as the appropriate government stamp and watermark.
5. We ask to meet with the government official responsible for the issuance of the land-use rights to confirm the terms of the agreement.
6. As with to our testing for fixed assets, we test payments to supporting documentation and bank statements—preferably obtained directly by us from the bank—and then trace the balances through the consolidation and published financial reports.

In our experience, most companies are not willing or able to provide all of the information we request, nor will we be able to perform each and every step in our process. Our ability to complete these procedures is often limited by factors like cost, time, poor corporate record-keeping, or government official availability. In the end, the strength of our conclusions tends to correlate directly to the access we're given.

Channel Checks

> Independent customer verification procedures, above and beyond those that would typically be performed in a US-style due diligence review, can provide valuable information about the validity of a company's underlying business.

We mentioned previously that counterfeit sales, when initially recorded, are often placed into an account receivable for a customer that either doesn't exist or has an arrangement with the company to return the goods at a later date with no money ever changing hands. There is a good chance that auditors will eventually uncover these types of transactions as accounts receivable get older and older with no collection. A small amount of bad debt is normal, but nonpayment trends should be easily identified by an experienced audit firm.

This is why companies may end up moving the balance into other accounts, such as cash, as discussed in the section on cash verification; fixed assets, as discussed in the section on fixed-asset verification; or other accounts on the balance sheet. We've designed specific procedures to test these accounts in an attempt to weed out the transactions and balances that are not real by independently confirming those that are. This grants some level of assurance that the balance was not simply shifted over to these other accounts.

In order to directly corroborate the company's sales and accounts receivable balances, we employ the following procedures:

1. We have the company provide us with a schedule of all sales, by customer, for the period(s) being tested.
2. We select a representative sample of customers and have the company arrange meetings with them. We ask to meet with either the chairman, the CEO, or the manager in charge of purchasing. In this way, we ensure that the individual we interview will be knowledgeable in the company's relationship to the company we're examining. We always prefer face-to-face meetings at the offices of the customer so that we can visually inspect the facilities, signage, employee count, and other readily visible information. We do this to better judge whether the business appears to be that which the company claims and also whether the business appears to be legitimately operating. If customers are scattered geographically and travel is not feasible

within the company's budget, we will hold the meetings over the phone.

3. We meet with customer representatives and have them verify (a) that they have a business relationship with the company, (b) the nature of the relationship and products bought from the company, and (c) whether there are any other relationships with the company, or its principals, outside of the standard supplier-customer dealings.
4. We then have the customer representative verify the amount of purchases made from the company during the period(s) being tested. Our preferred method for this validation is to have customers print a purchase log for us from their accounting system without knowing what the company's records indicate. However, because of privacy concerns, this request may not be granted. Alternatively, we will prepare a confirmation letter with a blank space for the purchases and ask the company to fill in the gross purchase amount for the period—and then chop the confirmation in our presence.

   If neither of these options is completed by the customer, we'll prepare a confirmation with the sales amounts already filled in and corresponding to what's reflected in the company's accounting system. We'll then ask customers to confirm that the amount reflected is accurate by comparing it to their records and then chopping the document. This last method is the least preferable, as customers may feel compelled to sign the confirmation even if the amount is incorrect. They tend to be more respectful of their business relationship with their supplier than of the confirmation process from an unknown third party.
5. In addition to our face-to-face meetings with customers, we perform independent fact checks on the customers to validate their existence. This includes basic tasks that we perform without the company's assistance, such as (a) performing a web search for customers to see if they're the subject of any news or Web coverage, (b) visiting the customers' website, if they have one, and reviewing facts like their business description and location,

(c) reviewing any publicly available financial statements, and (d) if our customer interview was done over the phone, calling the customer's main phone number, such as the one listed on their website, and asking to be connected with the interviewee to confirm that he or she actually works there.

We perform these procedures not only for a company's customers but also for their suppliers. If a company is inflating its revenue, it's a good bet it's also claiming purchases that don't exist. The reason companies do this is that auditors, analysts, and shareholders, in general, can easily compare a company's profit margins to those of competitors in the same industry. If the company does not show overstated purchases and a resulting cost of goods sold, its margins will be skewed. This raises red flags for outsiders. We've seen companies completely fabricate suppliers and purchases in an attempt to disguise sales fraud.

To verify suppliers, we perform similar procedures to the customer channel check. We have the company provide us with a list of suppliers and purchasers. We then perform interviews on a portion of this list using the same approach we employed for the company's customers.

Government Official Interviews

> In China, where the government is omnipresent in the business landscape, going directly to the government can be one of the most valuable due diligence weapons in the arsenal.

One additional and highly valuable service that's been well received by clients in our forensic due diligence assignments is the interviewing of government officials. We normally focus our efforts on local government officials because they're intimately familiar with the local economic and industrial environments. They also know the company's competitors and the willingness of the provincial and municipal governments to support our client's industry.

The purpose of interviewing local government officials is to obtain an understanding of the government's general attitude toward the company and identify any potential areas of concern or optimism with respect to the company's business. We attempt to speak to officials from different government disciplines. These areas would commonly include tax, commerce, industry, and environmental compliance.

When we speak to tax officials, we generally end up at a local branch office of the national tax bureau. Corporate taxes in China are legislated centrally out of Beijing but implemented through the thousands of local tax offices that act as extensions of the central tax bureau. Sample questions that we ask of tax officials include the following:

- Is the company subject to any special tax treatment, such as tax rebates or holidays?
- Has the company filed all of its tax returns in a timely fashion?
- Does the company have any unpaid tax liability?
- Have there been any tax audits or inspections of the company in recent years, and, if so, what was the outcome?
- What is your general opinion of the company?

We also visit the local office of the SAIC and interview the highest-ranked official available. The SAIC is responsible for corporate registration and administration. Sample questions that we ask the SAIC official include the following:

- Does the company have a validly issued business license?
- Has the company filed all SAIC reports in a timely fashion?
- Has an annual inspection been performed recently, and if so, what were the results?
- Are you aware of any government initiatives that may affect the company's business going forward?
- What is your general opinion of the company?

The environmental protection offices are responsible for issuing environmental approvals for new construction projects as well as inspecting required changes to current environmental laws that are required to be implemented by businesses. Sample questions that we ask an environmental official include:

- Is the company in violation of any environmental laws or regulations?
- Has the company filed all relevant environmental approval documents?
- What is your general opinion of the company?

The Quality and Technology Supervision Bureau is responsible for matters related to quality, measurements, entry-exit commodity inspection, entry-exit quarantine, entry-exit quarantine of plants and animals, and the approval of related licenses and standards. Among other things, it can issue organization code certificates and production licenses for certain controlled industrial products. For companies in industries where this bureau is relevant, we interview the official and ask the following:

- Does the company have a validly issued production license related to the products that it claims to manufacture?
- Is information on the company's organization code certificate accurate?
- Is the company in compliance with all laws and regulations of your bureau?
- What is your general opinion of the company?

The questions asked of each official will vary depending on the facts and circumstances of each company, its industry, its geographic location, and many other factors. There may also be industry-specific government bureaus that have authority over the operations of a company, and if material or relevant, we will request an interview with those officials on a case-by-case basis.

Chapter 12
Piercing the Great Wall

As we've seen, performing due diligence on a Chinese company can be extremely difficult. Evaluating a business, or investment opportunity in China requires a unique set of forensic due diligence tools in order to obtain the information necessary to identify unusual or noncompliant aspects of a business or situation. The techniques employed in Europe, Latin America, or even in other Asian countries may be wholly unsuccessful in providing the accurate data required to make an informed business judgment in China. As we've pointed out, being successful in the land of the dragon necessitates modifying one's existing forensic due diligence techniques to adapt to Chinese philosophical, cultural, and business realities.

Prior to December 1978, when China opened itself to conducting global trade, business in China was largely conducted internally, except for trade with the Soviet Union and Soviet Bloc countries. Unlike European nations, for example, which have been international trading partners for centuries, China only has three and a half decades of global foreign-trade experience. Most of what we know about Chinese business practices has been learned in that short amount of time. As a result, even companies that have long and successful histories in international trade but failed to understand this unique business environment have been carried out on their shield. In contrast, companies that have adopted the forensic due diligence techniques we discussed have been able to reap the financial rewards of conducting business in China's robust economic environment.

Many companies believe that due diligence is basically the same globally and that they can easily adjust for local differences. They therefore conduct their investigation and evaluation of a Chinese business much as they would a business in India, for example. We mention India because we once had the CEO of a US public company tell us, at a conference in New York, that he was conducting his own due diligence on a joint venture he was entering into in China. He was proud of the fact that he didn't use an outside firm, because due diligence, as he explained to us, was basically following a checklist. His comment was: "I just did a JV in India, I think I can easily handle one in China."

One year later, what do you think happened? You guessed it. Sales revenue decreased, vendor costs escalated, the company lost money, and the joint venture collapsed. The fact was, this CEO didn't know what he was getting himself into because he didn't have the right evaluation tools, methodology, and understanding of the Chinese government and business environment. He also didn't have current information on what was actually happening within his joint venture in order to make informed decisions.

We mention this because we feel that the information contained in *Piercing the Great Wall of Corporate China* will not only provide you with the tools necessary to avoid a similar fate but also enable you to know the details of the situation in which you're about to engage. That's not to say, as we discussed, that fraud and misconduct by Chinese businesses don't occur. They do. But in quite a few instances these accusations have been based on foreign partners' lack of sophistication in knowing what they're stepping into. Simply put, both sides weren't on the same page when they entered into the agreement and each had different expectations.

Sometimes stories of joint ventures or investments going astray have deterred people from conducting business in the land of the dragon. But for the business community, ignoring China would be a mistake. China's economy continues to show exponential growth. It's the world's second largest economy and, in a little more than a decade, will soon become its largest. At that point, it will also be the world's largest importer and exporter of goods. As a result, foreign companies are eager to increase their services, manufacturing, and commerce within the land of the dragon. They've decided that China has to be an integral part of future growth, which has resulted in an increase in cross-border transactions. These companies require specialized forensic due diligence procedures to provide them with transparency, and the ability to pierce the great wall of secrecy surrounding most Chinese businesses.

One reason that specialized forensic due diligence procedures are necessary within China is because independent verification of information is difficult. The government views requests for corporate data by someone outside the company—even with the company's permission—as unnecessary and suspicious. This is because the Chinese bureaucracy believes that the company should already have this information. Therefore, why would the company ask the government for what it already received?

This is one reason why, unlike in most Western countries where auditors routinely ask for and receive such information from third parties, obtaining similar information within China may be extremely difficult without the knowledge and procedures necessary to work within the government's bureaucratic framework. In addition, many institutions, especially at the local level, feel there's little reason to store historical data for extended periods of time, which may be as short as six months. This again makes it difficult to independently verify information provided by the entity on which forensic due diligence is being conducted.

This situation is seldom encountered in more Westernized countries. However, as we've noted, there are procedures that can be employed to independently verify historical data. In the two examples of the government's reluctance to hand over corporate data and an institution's inability to provide third-party verification, a knowledge of Chinese bureaucracy and business practices, such as we've provided, will in many cases allow one to obtain and independently verify such data.

Taking the information we've provided will allow you to conduct comprehensive forensic due diligence on a Chinese business entity. Putting this data together in a report should enable you to come up with one that's as detailed as the Thornhill Capital forensic due diligence report in Appendix A. This report utilizes the same information and procedures we've discussed for performing forensic due diligence on a Chinese company.

We firmly believe that comprehending the singularities of Chinese businesses as relates to forensic due diligence will enable one to successfully pierce the great wall of corporate China and gain an exacting view of the entity they're evaluating. It will also enable one to avoid the pitfalls and failures of those who don't have the knowledge base necessary to be successful in the land of the dragon.

Being successful in China isn't an accident. It's the result of preparation and having the tools necessary to successfully perform forensic due diligence on a Chinese company. In *Piercing the Great Wall of Corporate China*, we provide you with the tools necessary to breach the wall.

APPENDIX A

Sample Due Diligence Report

Due Diligence Report

Lihua International, Inc.

Prepared by: Thornhill Capital LLC
Date: August 9, 2011

Contents

Introduction

Thornhill Capital LLC ("Thornhill") has prepared this Due Diligence Report on behalf of an unrelated third party. The subject entity is Lihua International, Inc. ("Lihua International"), and its operating subsidiaries Danyang Lihua Electron Co., Ltd. ("Lihua Electron") and Jiangsu Lihua Copper Industry Co., Ltd. ("Lihua Copper"). Collectively, this report refers to the combined entity as the "Company." All of the business of the two operating entities, Lihua Electron and Lihua Copper, is conducted in China.

Thornhill was engaged to visit the Company's facilities to attempt to identify any unusual accounting or business practices not in accordance with United States (the "US") generally accepted accounting principles ("US GAAP"). No information regarding our findings was provided prior to the publishing of this report.

Scope of Work

From July 12-16, and August 3-4, 2011, Thornhill visited the Company's facilities, located in Danyang, Jiangsu Province, People's Republic of China ("China" or the "PRC"). At the Company's facilities, we reviewed legal and accounting documentation, toured the production plants, and interviewed the following Company personnel:

- COO, Secretary and Director: Wang Yaying
- CFO and Treasurer: Yu Yang
- Financial Manager: Chu Chunming

Also, as further described in this report, we independently interviewed local government officials, customers, and suppliers, and directly obtained documentation from banking institutions and government tax offices in China.

Please refer to Exhibit A hereto for biographical information on the Thornhill team involved in compiling this report.

Corporate Structure

Lihua International acquired the operations of Lihua Electron and Lihua Copper on October 31, 2008 through a reverse acquisition of Ally Profit Investments, Ltd. ("Ally Profit"), a British Virgin Islands ("BVI") holding company that owns 100% of Lihua Holdings Ltd. ("Lihua Holdings"), a Hong Kong holding company, which in turn owns Lihua Electron and Lihua Copper. The following diagram reflects this corporate structure, which is common to Chinese reverse mergers and required to comply with Chinese laws:

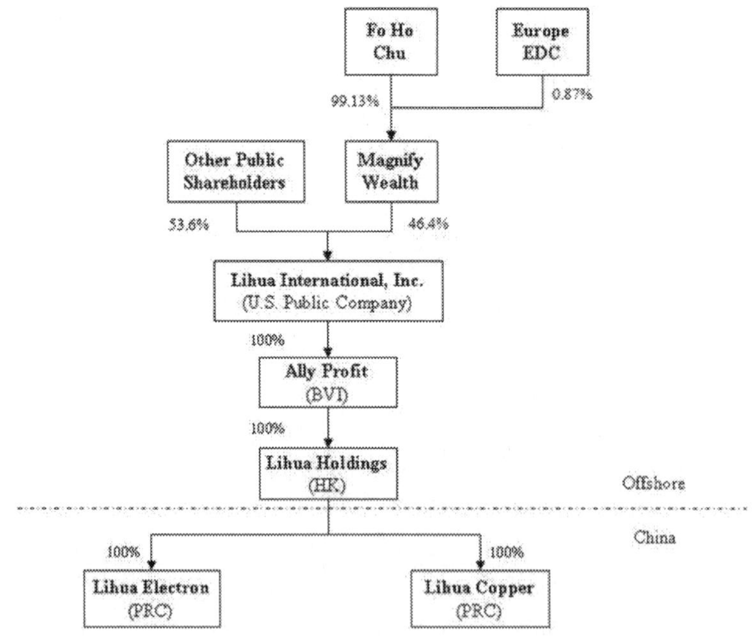

The capital structure of the PRC operating entities is as follows:

	Lihua Copper	**Lihua Electron**
Incorporation Date	August 31, 2007	December 30, 1999
Location	Wuxing Industrial Development Zone, Houxiang Township, Danyang, Jiangsu Province, China	Wuxing Industrial Development Zone, Houxiang Township, Danyang, Jiangsu Province, China
Legal Representative	Zhu Jianhua (President, CEO, and Chairman of the Board of Lihua International)	Zhu Jianhua (President, CEO, and Chairman of the Board of Lihua International)
Shareholder	Lihua Holdings Limited	Lihua Holdings Limited
Registered capital		
- Total	US$65 million	US$10.5 million
- Contributed to date	US$46 million	US$10.5 million
- Deadline for remaining contribution	May 5, 2012	n/a

Business description	Production and sale of refined copper rod, bimetal materials and recycled copper anode plate	Production and sale of electric wire and cable, copper wire, copper clad aluminum wire, copper clad aluminum special electromagnetic wire

We independently verified the above described legal and capital information to capital verification reports provided directly to us from the State Administration for Industry and Commerce when we visited their offices on July 14, 2011.

Operational Overview

Overview

The following description of the Company's business and operations is intended to be a high-level summary for the purpose of providing context to this report. A complete description of the Company's business can be found in the Company's Annual Report on Form 10-K as filed with the US Securities and Exchange Commission (the "SEC") on March 14, 2011.

The Company is a vertically integrated designer, manufacturer, marketer and distributor of refined copper products including copper anode, copper rod, pure superfine copper wire, and copper-clad aluminum ("CCA") superfine wire, which is an alternative to pure superfine copper wire. The Company also uses recycled scrap copper as a raw material to produce refined copper products including copper anode and copper rod. Copper anode is the raw material for copper cathode, which is the fundamental building block for most pure copper products. The Company primarily uses copper rods internally to produce pure copper superfine wire. Because of its high electrical conductivity, pure copper wire is used in many components in a wide variety of motorized and electrical appliances such as dishwashers, microwaves and automobiles. In most instances, CCA wire and recycled scrap copper rod and wire products are a less costly substitute for pure copper wire products.

The Company sells copper anode primarily to a few copper conglomerates. The Company sells wire products directly to manufacturers in the consumer electronics, white goods, automotive, utility, telecommunications and specialty cable industries and to distributors in the wire and cable industries. In the PRC, the market for copper products, which includes the copper wire industry, is large and growing. As a result, essentially all of the Company's product sales are to domestic customers in the PRC.

Products

The Company manufactures the following products:

Copper Anode

An anode is an electrode through which electric current flows into a polarized electrical device. Copper anode is the raw material for the production of copper cathode, which is the fundamental building block of most pure copper products. In July 2010, the Company completed construction of a scrap copper smelter dedicated to the production of copper anode, and started manufacturing and selling copper anode in August 2010, mainly to large copper entities which produce and sell copper cathode to domestic PRC copper products manufacturers.

Copper Rod and Copper Wire

The Company began manufacturing copper rod in March 2009, using scrap copper as the raw material to manufacture and sell copper rods. In addition, the Company produces cable and copper magnet wire from copper rods.

Copper rod based wire products have various uses, including telephone drop wire and conductors, electric utilities; transmission lines, grid wire, fence and structured grounds, magnet wire, battery cables, automotive wiring harnesses, and radio frequency shielding.

The superfine pure copper wire the Company manufactures is stretched from copper rod. Superfine wire is produced and distributed in the following forms:

- *Fine wire* – sold to smaller wire manufacturers for further processing

- *Magnet wire* – can be fine or super fine and is the basic building block of a wide range of motorized appliances and is mainly used for its electrical conductivity
- *Tin plated wire* – mainly used for the transmission of audio and visual signals

Copper Clad Aluminum (CCA) Superfine Wire

CCA is an electrical conductor consisting of an outer sleeve of copper that is metallurgically bonded to a solid aluminum core. Over the past five years, CCA has become a viable and popular alternative to pure copper wire. In comparison with solid copper wire, CCA raw material costs are generally 35% to 40% lower. Since aluminum accounts for approximately eighty-six percent (86%) by volume of CCA wire, each ton of CCA wire can yield 2.5 times the length of each ton of solid copper wire. The Company's CCA products are a cost effective substitute for pure copper wire in a wide variety of applications such as wire and cable, consumer electronic products, white goods, automotive parts, utility applications, telecommunications, and specialty cables.

The Company produces CCA wire with a line diameter in the range of 0.03 mm to 0.18 mm. CCA is produced and distributed in the following forms:

- *Fine wire* – sold to smaller wire manufacturers for further processing;
- *Magnet wire* – can be fine or super fine and is the basic building block of a wide range of motorized appliances and is mainly used for its electrical conductivity.
- *Tin plated wire* – mainly used for the transmission of audio and visual signals.

Facilities

The Company's manufacturing facilities are comprised of the following:

	Lihua Electron	Lihua Copper - Existing Facility	Lihua Copper - New Facility
Location	Danyang	Danyang	Danyang
Began construction	Mar-99	Mar-08	Nov-10
Began production	Dec-99 (a)	Mar-09	Estimated end of Q3 2011
Capacity (metric tons per year)	CCA wire-7,500	Copper refinery-50,000	Copper refinery-50,000
		Copper wire-20,000	
Site area (square meters)			
Total land area	10,471	66,666	120,000
Office building area	1,681	10,026	-
Plant area	7,144	22,928	21,484

(a) The Company built its plant in 1999, and it was used for the production of copper connectors (such as plug/socket copper accessories) from 1999 to January 2006, at which time production of CCA was undertaken

We reviewed land use certificates and property ownership certificates for the two operational facilities. The certificates are validly issued, agree with the date outlined above, and agree with our visual inspection of each facility.

The land use and property ownership certificates for the new facility will not be issued until the project has been completed. We reviewed the following documents relating to the construction and environmental approvals of this facility:

- Approval document issued by the Development and Reform Commission of Danyang for new construction project production line with annual capacity of 170,000 tons of recycled copper and copper anode, issued on August 11, 2010. The approval document is for a total of 170,000 tons capacity, but the initial expansion of the plant covers only 50,000 tons. So the Company is pre-approved to perform additional expansion of up to 120,000 tons of capacity.

- Examination and approval of the Environmental Impact Statement for the new construction project with annual capacity of 170,000 tons of recycled copper and copper anode, issued by the Environment Protection Bureau on August 2, 2010

- Preliminary examining opinions on the land used for the project with an annual capacity of 170,000 tons of recycled copper and copper anode, issued by the Land and Resources Bureau on July 23, 2010

In addition to the above manufacturing facilities, the Company maintains the following remote sales offices:

	Office name	**Address**
1	Foshan Office 1	Liangdong Industrial Zone, Liangqingtang, Dali Township, Nanhai District, Foshan, Guangdong
2	Foshan Office 2	Shop 210, Building # 2, Poly Water City, No. 20, Denghu West Road, Guicheng Sub-district, Nanhai District, Foshan, Guangdong

3	Foshan Office 3	Shop 302, Building # 1, Poly Water City, No. 20, Denghu West Road, Guicheng Sub-district, Nanhai District, Foshan, Guangdong
4	Zhonshan Office	Street Shop 6, Business-living Building # 6, No. 3, Xiaolan Middle Road, Zhongshan
5	Taizhou Office	Close to 104 National Road, Daxi Township, Wenling County, Taizhou, Zhejiang
6	Fuan Office	No. 47, Jinyuan New Road, Chengyang Township, Fuan
7	Shengzhou Office	No. 25, Electronic Machine Commercial Market, Changle Township, Shengzhou
8	Anhui Office	Tongling, Anhui
9	Shunde Office and Sanshui Office	Shundeng District, Foshan
10	Shandong Office	Mouping District, Yantai, Shandong

Employees

The Company provided the following table showing the number of employees by function (note that the Company's 2010 Form 10-K states that they had 346 employees as of December, 31, 2010):

	Lihua Electron	**Lihua Copper**	**Total**
Administrative	36	34	70
Sales	30	12	42
Production management	18	9	27
Production	137	74	211
	221	129	350

In order to verify the personnel number, we examined each company's payroll forms and employee insurance payment lists, and checked the data for randomly selected sample months of December 2009, December 2010 and May 2011. Our findings were as follows:

- December 2009: the number of employees in the payroll form totaled 308, and the number of employees on the insurance payment list totaled 304

- December 2010: the number of employees in the payroll form totaled 342, and the number of employees on the insurance payment list totaled 339

- May 2011: the number of employees in the payroll form totaled 349, and the number of employees on the insurance payment list totaled 346

We did not deem these differences to be material.

Additionally, we counted the number of production employees for reasonableness with the following results:

- During our initial visit in July 2011, both Lihua Copper furnaces were down for repair (see section entitled "Copper Rod Smelter Down for Repair/Upgrade"), and accordingly there was little to no production activity and few workers present. During our second visit in August 2011, however, one furnace was operational and we noted approximately 40 employees on the factory floor. The employees are divided into five groups: furnace burning team, materials charging team, discharging team, packing team, and transporting team. Each team consists of 7-8 individuals, for a total of 35-40 production employees per shift. Lihua Copper operates two 12-hour shifts, for a total of 70-80 employees, making our observations consistent with the number of production employees in Lihua Copper (74) provided by the Company.

- We also toured the production area for Lihua Electron and counted 66 employees on the floor, comprised of packaging employees, enameling employees, wiredrawing employees, annealing employees, electricians, and mechanics. Lihua Electron operates two 12-hour shifts, for a total of approximately 132 production employees according to our sample account, which is consistent with the number of production employees in Lihua Electron (137) provided by the Company.

We also confirmed that the number of administrative employees was reasonably stated through observation:

- For Lihua Copper, we counted 34 administrative staff as follows: 4 security guards (total of 8 when multiplied by 2 shifts, plus there are an additional 3 in the dormitories that we did not observe), 5 logistical employees in the cafeteria (there are 9 logistical employees in total, 5 were working and 4 were off), 2 employees in the infrastructure project division, 2 employees in the IT department, 4 employees in the vehicle team office, 2 employees in the personnel department, and 4 employees in the financial department. The total was 34, which agrees to the number provided.

- For Lihua Electron, we counted 2 logistical employees, 2 security guards (times 2 shifts equals 4 total), 6 employees in the equipment department, 3 in the purchase department, 3 in the financial department, 10 vehicle guards, and 8 executives. The total was 36, which agrees to the number provided.

Based on this approach we concluded that the number of employees is accurately reflected.

Licenses and Certificates

Part of our due diligence review included examining the licenses and certificates issued by various PRC governmental authorities that the Company is required to obtain in order to operate its businesses in accordance with PRC law. Our findings are described below.

Lihua Electron

Business license
Issued by: Danyang Administrative Bureau of Industry and Commerce
Term: December 31, 1999 - December 29, 2014
The annual examination of 2010 has been passed

Organization code certificate
Issued by: Danyang Supervision Bureau of Quality and Technology
Term: June 18, 2009 - June 17, 2013
The annual examination of 2010 has been passed.

Tax registration certificate
Issued by: Danyang National Tax Bureau and Danyang Local Tax Bureau
Status: Lihua Electron is categorized as a general VAT taxpayer (no special exceptions, exemptions, or preferential tax rates)

Production license for industrial products
Issued by: General Administration of Quality Supervision, Inspection and Quarantine
Term: January 15, 2009 - January 14, 2014

Application for environmental protection acceptance of project completion (for technological upgrading project of special electromagnetic wire production line)
Approved by: Danyang Houxiang Township Environmental Protection Office
Examined and approved on: January 8, 2009

Notice of approval of capital increase of annual production of 6,000-ton copper clad special electromagnetic wire
Approved by: Danyang Development and Reform Commission
Approved on: June 10, 2007

Lihua Copper

Business license
Issued by: Danyang Administrative Bureau of Industry and Commerce
Term: August 31, 2007 - August 30, 2018
The annual examination of 2010 has been passed.

Organization code certificate
Issued by: Danyang Supervision Bureau of Quality and Technology
Term: November 15, 2007 - November 14, 2011
The annual examination of 2010 has been passed.

Tax registration certificate
Issued by: Danyang National Tax Bureau and Danyang Local Tax Bureau
Status: Lihua Electron is categorized as a general VAT taxpayer (no special exceptions, exemptions, or preferential tax rates)

Production license for industrial products
We noted that Lihua Copper does not have a production license for industrial products, which is a license required by the PRC government for production of certain types of controlled products. The Company explained that their products do not require a production license for industrial products. In order to verify this, we went to the Beijing Quality Supervision Bureau's official list of industrial products for which a production license is required (located at http://www.bjtsb.gov.cn/infoview.asp?ViewID=8388; copy of the official list also attached hereto as Exhibit B).

The only item that resembles the Company's products on this list is Item 41, "copper and copper alloy tubes." However, by its literal definition this product category encompasses hollow copper tubes, and does not include the Company's products which are copper rods and anode plates. We note that none of the other categories are relevant to the Company's products. This supports the Company's position that no production license for industrial products is required.

Registration license for domestic consignees of imported solid waste as raw materials
Issued by: General Administration of Quality Supervision, Inspection and Quarantine
Term: November 23, 2010- November 22, 2013

Application for environmental protection acceptance of project completion (process and production project of non-ferrous metal – refined copper rod and oxygen-free copper rod and bimetal materials):
Examined and approved on: January 8, 2009
Approved by: Danyang Houxiang Township Economic Service Center, Danyang Houxiang Township Environmental Protection Supervision Office, Danyang Environmental Protection Bureau

Notice of approval for new construction project of 60,000-ton non-ferrous metals (refined copper rod and oxygen-free copper rod), bimetal materials (special electromagnetic wire)
Approved on: July 23, 2008
Approved by: Danyang Development and Reform Commission

Reply on approval of new construction project production line with annual production of 170,000 tons of recycled copper and copper anode
Approved on: August 11, 2010
Approved by: Danyang Development and Reform Commission

We noted that each of the original business licenses, organization code certificates, and tax registration certificates that we reviewed showed a watermark or shading that is put in place by the government as a fraud-protection device.

Conclusion

It is not standard practices for government offices to issue copies of licenses, similar to how they would issue a copy of a tax report, for verification purposes. To gain further comfort that the licenses provided by the Company were authentic, we interviewed government officials from the Danyang Administrative Bureau of Industry and Commerce, and the Danyang Houxiang Township Environmental Protection Office. Both officials confirmed that the Company was current on all of its verifications required to be filed with their offices (see section entitled "Interviews with Government Officials" for additional details of our conversations). We did not speak with each government office issuing certificates or licenses listed above, but based on our sample confirmations of the above licenses, as well as the presence of the government watermarks on the original licenses that we reviewed, it appears reasonable that the Company has received and maintained all appropriate licenses required to operate their current business.

Tax Reconciliation

Background

Perhaps the most common issue that arises for Chinese companies listed in the US is an inability to reconcile tax reports filed with the PRC government to audited US GAAP results filed with the SEC. This is usually a tax avoidance strategy or an intent to misrepresent results in an attempt to increase a company's valuation and their chance to raise money in the US.

The China State Administration for Industry and Commerce ("SAIC") is the Chinese government agency responsible for issuing and renewing companies' business licenses. Foreign invested enterprises are required to file annual PRC GAAP audited results with the SAIC. Each of the Company's subsidiaries electronically files its annual SAIC reports to a secured SAIC database, which is shared by various other tax authorities including the State Administration of Taxation ("SAT"), for annual review and inspection. Each subsidiary makes quarterly estimated SAT tax payments throughout the year, and then files an income tax return with the SAT to true up the amount owed at year-end.

The Company's SAIC reports are prepared in accordance with Chinese accounting rules and policies, and reflect financial information relating to Lihua Electron and Lihua Copper on an unconsolidated basis. Accordingly, there are certain intercompany and US GAAP adjustments that are made to the financial statements during the US GAAP consolidation that are appropriately not reflected in the SAIC filings. These adjustments generally include intercompany sales (which are not included in the individual subsidiary SAIC reports since each company files individually and must report all sales, even to entities owned by the same parent company), costs incurred by offshore holding companies, and US GAAP non-cash adjustments such as entries related to offshore financing transactions, and valuation of related debt, equity and derivative instruments based in the equity of the offshore holding corporations. In other words, there are legitimate, and often material, reconciling items that must be taken into consideration when bridging from SAIC to US GAAP reported financial results.

Our general process for reconciling a Chinese company's tax filings to its audited financial information reported in its public filings is as follows:

1. Obtain and review management account financial data that agrees to what the company purports to have filed with the SAIC.
2. Independently obtain tax reports filed with the SAIC by visiting the local tax office, observing the filing in the computer system, and observing the filing being printed by the tax official.

3. Independently verify amounts filed with the SAT. This task is more problematic than verifying SAIC reports, since SAT policy is not to provide copies of filings. The Company provides us with a stamped copy of what they filed with the SAT. To verify authenticity, we can use one of the following methods:
    a. If the company files its income tax returns online using the SAT's secure database, we log in using the company's access codes, and review and print filed data directly from the government website.
    b. For manual income tax filers, we cross-reference (i) all financial information in the company-provided SAT tax return to the independently obtained SAIC report, (ii) sales on the SAT income tax report to stamped filed value added tax ("VAT") returns provided by the company, and (iii) sales on the SAT income tax return to sales in the online government VAT filing system, using the company's login information (if the company is an online filer). Manual filers provide the lowest level of direct independent verification since we are unable to directly obtain the filed report from the filing agency. But these cross-references to various data points, including to independently verified SAIC reports, when combined with independent payment verification outlined in Step #6 below.
4. Agree or reconcile balance sheet and income statement published in SAIC reports, SAT returns, and VAT returns to management accounts for each subsidiary.
5. Obtain consolidation worksheet from audit file that shows the combination of the management accounts of all subsidiaries, plus US GAAP eliminations, plus US GAAP adjusting journal entries, and conversion from local currency to US dollars. We then agree the US dollar combined and adjusted financials to SEC filings (10-K or 10-Q).
6. Finally, we verify all tax payments shown on the declaration forms, by personally visiting the banks from which the payments

were made (with a company representative) and observe the printing of the bank statements reflecting the payment.

Findings

Step 1 – Obtain management accounts
The financial department of the Company provided us with PRC GAAP management account trial balances, and US GAAP consolidating and eliminating worksheets prior to our arrival.

Step 2 – Verify SAIC reports
On July 14, 2011, we independently obtained the data filed with the SAIC by visiting the Danyang SAIC branch. We met with Lu Hui from the Data Inquiry Dept of Danyang Industrial and Commercial Bureau. SAIC filings for years ended December 31, 2008 and 2009 for each of Lihua Copper and Lihua Electron were printed from SAIC's computer system while we observed. For 2010 filings, the SAIC personnel explained to us that the companies' filings had only recently been made, and therefore had not been reviewed by SAIC staff and entered into the database. Therefore, no data existed in the SAIC system for printing for 2010. However, to satisfy our independence requirement, SAIC personnel manually copied the 2010 return from the files of Lihua Copper and Lihua Electron while we observed.

Step 3 – Verify SAT reports
To further verify the companies' data filed with the SAT, we asked the Company to login to the online SAT database so we could print returns. The Company informed us it did not use SAT online declaration system, instead each subsidiary elects to file returns manually. The Company's rationale for not using the online filing system is that they do not trust the network security of the online system, electing instead to manually file at the tax office. So we proceeded to step 3(b), cross-referencing information from the Company-provided SAT return to the independently-obtained SAIC report, and to the Company's VAT filings.

The SAT filings agreed to the SAIC reports with only minor differences. All variances were less than 1% for individual line items and in the aggregate, with the exception of the 2009 Lihua Copper returns. On these returns, net income varied between the SAIC and SAT reports by RMB 1.4 million, or about 2.9%, and income tax expense by RMB 0.7 million, or about 4.7%. The variances are caused by adjustments made by the Chinese audit firm during the Chinese GAAP audit of the financials included in the SAIC report, after the filing of the SAT return. Because the SAT return was filed in January 2010, and the Chinese audit was not completed until April 2010, certain audit adjustments were not reflected in the SAT return. These adjustments relate to an inventory write-up of approximately RMB 2.4 million, offset by other additional expense adjustments of about RMB 1 million. On a consolidated basis, the difference in net income represents about 1.2% of net income reported in the Company's 2009 US GAAP audited financials. We do not deem these differences to be material. Refer to Exhibit C hereto for a complete reconciliation and comparison of Lihua Copper and Lihua Electron management accounts, VAT filings, SAT returns, and SAIC reports for years 2008-2010.

The Company files its VAT returns through the government's online system, so we logged on using their access codes. We noted that, because of the nature of the government system, only historical data between December 2010 and June 2011 was available. The VAT system only allows access to filing information for the last month of previous year, and for every month of current year.

Because the data available in the online system did not cover an entire fiscal year, we were unable to verify the sales data in the system to any filed returns. However, we were able to verify that the sales from the online system agreed to the Company's management accounts for the six months ended June 30, 2011. These management accounts have been provided to the Company's auditors for the second quarter review. This lends some credibility to the Company's VAT data. We then agreed total sales from the VAT filings from 2008-2010 provided by the Company to the SAT filings, without any issues.

As a manual SAT filer, the Company falls into the bucket offering the least independent verification of the accuracy of their SAT filings. However, we were able to gain a substantial amount of comfort regarding the validity of the SAT returns based on the fact that (i) the SAT returns provided by the Company agreed to the independently obtained SAIC reports, (ii) current VAT data obtained directly by us from the government database agreed to management accounts provided to auditors to be used in SEC reports, and (iii) sales data in the SAT returns agreed to filed VAT returns provided by the Company.

<u>Step 4 – reconcile government filings to management accounts</u>
We then began the reconciliation process, comparing the management accounts to the SAIC reports, SAT returns, and VAT returns. We noted the following discrepancies:

- The Lihua Copper 2008 SAIC report varied materially in certain respects from the management accounts, as follows (see Exhibit C-4 for details by line item):
    - While total assets only varied by about RMB 1.3 million on a total balance sheet of RMB 110 million (about 1.2%), the individual line items were materially different. The SAIC return classifies a substantial amount of assets as prepayments and Other Accounts Receivable (usually a catch-all asset holding account for Chinese companies), both current assets. On the management accounts, however, the majority of the assets are in the form of long term assets like construction in progress and intangible assets.
    - The SAIC report reflects cash balances of only RMB 1.9 million, while the management accounts show RMB 10.8 million in cash.
    - The management accounts reflect a net loss of RMB 403,876, and the neither the SAT return nor the SAIC

report reflects any operations in 2008. Since the actual management account result was a loss, there was no unreported tax liability.

  - We asked management about the discrepancy, and their response was that Lihua Copper had just been established in 2008, and in order to make a quick declaration to the SAIC in order to obtain the business license annual examination, the financials in the report were prepared based on incomplete data. We did note, however, that the Chinese audit report was not issued until May 2009, which is sufficient time after year end to prepare accurate accounts, especially considering that the results consisted only of start-up costs.
  - We also noted that the Company later revised the 2008 balance sheet data in the prior year comparative column of its 2009 SAIC report for Lihua Copper. The comparative prior year balance sheet data in the 2009 report agree to the management accounts. The comparative prior year income statement data was never corrected.

- Net income reported on the Lihua Copper's 2009 SAIC report varied from the management accounts by RMB 954,000, or 2%. The immaterial differences are due to timing recognition differences for book and tax purposes, and to classification differences between PRC tax reporting and book reporting under US GAAP. We did not deem this difference to be material.
- In all other cases, we noted only immaterial variances between the management accounts and the filed returns, in no case greater than 1% of the individual line item in question.

Refer to Exhibit C hereto for a complete reconciliation and comparison of Lihua Copper and Lihua Electron management accounts, VAT filings, SAT returns, and SAIC reports for years 2008-2010.

Step 5 – reconcile management accounts to SEC filings

Our next step was to trace the management accounts through the consolidation, elimination, and currency conversion process. We reviewed the Company's consolidation worksheet for each of the years ended December 31, 2008, 2009, and 2010, as provided to us by the finance department. We traced formulae through the worksheet to ensure that it was properly compiling information. We also tested currency conversion rates for reasonableness. We noted no issues with the mechanical workings of the consolidation. We then agreed the final consolidated US GAAP financial statements to the statements that were published in the Company's annual reports on Form 10-K, located in the SEC's Edgar filing database. We did not independently verify any information related to offshore companies Lihua Holdings (HK), Ally Profit (BVI), or Lihua International, Inc. (US).

Step 6 – verify tax payments

Our final step in verifying that the Company's tax returns are genuine is to trace payment of tax payable as shown on the tax return to the bank statement showing the cash disbursement. The accounts from which the tax payments were made were both located at Agricultural Bank of China, Danyang Houxiang Branch. There was one account for Lihua Copper and one for Lihua Electron.

We went to the bank accompanied by Company personnel to authorize the bank to issue the statements to us. The bank personnel responsible for printing statements was Dou Wenjie, Business Manager of Agricultural Bank of China, Danyang Houxiang Branch.

We acquired the two subsidiaries' bank statements for the period from January 2010 to June 2011 (as far back as the bank branch was able to give us). We verified tax payments on the bank statements, which were consistent with those in the SAIC and SAT reports for fiscal year 2010, without exception. For tax payments related to fiscal years 2008 and 2009, we verified tax payments to copies of bank statements provided to us by the Company, without exception. We did not obtain the 2008-2009 bank statements independently, as the cash verification process, aside from the Agricultural Bank of China Danyang Houxiang Branch accounts detailed in this section, was outside of the scope of this report (see section entitled "Cash Verification").

Conclusion

Based on the procedures outlined herein, we have concluded that it is unlikely that the Company has filed incorrect SAT or SAIC reports, or provided us with false reports that do not agree to the actual reports filed.

Our most compelling evidence is that we independently visited the local SAIC office and observed the SAIC data in the government computer system, and also observed the printing of the reports. The reports reconcile to the Company's financial information reported to the SEC.

Also providing strong support to the verification process is the fact that we independently obtained bank statements on location at the bank for the accounts from which tax payments were made related to tax year 2010. We verified that tax payments agreed from the bank statements to the tax reports. We also traced 2008 and 2009 tax payments to copies of bank statements provided by the Company.

The weakest objective evidence in the process relates to the verification of the SAT returns. Since the Company files its returns manually and the SAT office does not release filed reports to outside parties, we were required to apply alternative verification procedures. We agreed the SAT reports provided by the Company to the independent SAIC reports (which in turn reconciled to the audited US GAAP results), verified that VAT data filed with the government agreed to the Company's data use for US public filings, and agreed sales from the SAT reports to filed VAT returns.

While we did note the discrepancies described in this section between management accounts and the government filings, the differences due to Chinese GAAP audit adjustments were not considered material. The differences relating to Lihua Copper in 2008, while material in the original filing on a line item basis, were corrected in the comparative column of the 2009 SAIC report, and did not affect the Company's tax liability since the unreported income statement result was a loss.

Recommendations

In order to most efficiently process tax filings in compliance with both PRC and US tax, legal, and securities regulations, the Company should consider utilizing the online system for filing its SAT returns. Not only is this method more efficient, as it uploads data directly into the government database, but it also provides a readily available objective verification of the validity of the filing, as a third party can easily log in to the system using the Company's access codes and download returns directly from the government. Combined with the other forms of independent verification described herein, having direct access to the government database would allow a third party to quickly and easily authenticate the Company's tax filings and payments with very little potential for misstatement.

Cash Verification

The process of verifying the cash balances did not fall within the scope of our due diligence report. The Company's board of directors informed us that, prior to our engagement, the Company had already engaged a separate firm to provide the cash verification service. Accordingly, we did not perform any services related to verifying cash balances reflected on the Company's audited balance sheets, other than verification of tax payments as described in the section entitled "Tax Reconciliation."

Interviews with Government Officials

As part of our due diligence review, we met with various government officials familiar with the Company and its operations. The purpose of these meetings was to obtain an understanding of the government's general attitude toward the Company, and identify any potential areas of concern or optimism with respect to the Company's business. We attempted to speak to officials from different government disciplines (mainly tax, commerce/industry, and environment for manufacturing companies) and ask about the Company's current position, prospects, compliance, and any other matters that they may deem relevant.

Following is a summary of our discussions relative to the Company. All officials interviewed discussed the combined operations of Lihua Copper and Lihua Electron.

Deputy Chief of Danyang National Tax Bureau: Mr. Wu Hongwei

"The Company is a key local enterprise, and tax authorities pay attention to its development and also believe it can realize substantial growth."

"The Company always pays taxes according to the tax law and has a good reputation. Currently we do not find it has any unpaid tax and no special tax inspection of the Company has occurred in recent years."

Director of Danyang Houxiang Township Industrial and Commercial Office: Mr. Liu Guoqiang

"The Company always conducts lawful operations and its certificates required by SAIC are all in compliance."

"According to the SAIC's requirements, an annual inspection of the Company is conducted and the inspection work mainly involves trademark usage, registered capital usage, and compliance with Contract Law. To date, no behaviors violating the laws and regulations have been found."

<u>Director of Danyang Houxiang Township Environmental Protection Office: Mr. Tang Yibo</u>

"The Company's relevant required documents are complete, and its production meets the requirements of relevant environmental laws and regulations."

"No behaviors violating environmental laws and regulations have been found."

Channel Checks

Procedures

In order to verify the existence of key customers and suppliers, as well as the level of business purportedly being executed with them, we routinely perform channel checks. This involves interviewing critical customers and suppliers to verify that they do business with the Company, that the amounts of purchases/sales in the Company's records are consistent with the customer's/supplier's records, to obtain their opinion about the Company, and to identify any other concerns or issues that the customer/supplier has with the Company. We chose the largest customers and suppliers in each period in order to give us at least 80% coverage of the individual subsidiary's sales or purchases and 50% of overall sales or purchases, or where sales or purchase were not concentrated, we tested a maximum of 10 samples.

In addition, since contact information for the customers and suppliers was provided by the Company, we randomly selected certain customers and suppliers for independent verification of contact information. For these companies, we looked up their main phone number online, then called the main number and asked to be routed to, or given the direct mobile number, of the individual that we interviewed. We then spoke to these individuals again to re-confirm that they worked for the customer or supplier. Customer or suppliers that we verified in this manner are denoted in the tables that follow. Contact names, addresses, and phone numbers of customers and suppliers have been withheld from this report, but are available upon request.

We directly called each of the following suppliers of Lihua Electron:

Supplier Name	Verified Contact
Jiangsu Lihua Copper Co., Ltd.(a)	X
Changzhou Suyun Electric Co., Ltd.	
Changzhou Minghao New Metal Material Co., Ltd.	X

(a) Represents intercompany transactions. We spoke with the contact person at Lihua Copper and also verified the purchases to sales accounting records of Lihua Copper
(b) The above suppliers represented 86% and 82% of Lihua Electron's purchases in 2011 and 2010, respectively

We directly called each of the following suppliers of Lihua Copper:

Supplier Name	Verified Contact
Zhaoqing Golden Trumpet Shell Recycling Co., Ltd.	
Foshan Nanhai Tianyuanhe Metal Recycling Co., Ltd.	X
Sihui Yian Renewable Resources Co., Ltd.	
Foshan Nanhai Meiyada Metal Recycling Co., Ltd.	X
Foshan Nanhai Tongding Metal Co., Ltd.	
Foshan Wanyuye Import and Export Co., Ltd.	

(a) The above suppliers represented 87% and 55% of Lihua Copper's purchases in 2011 and 2010, respectively

We directly called each of the following customers of Lihua Electron:

Customer name	Verified Contact
Jiangsu Shangshang Cable Group Co., Ltd.	X
Zhongshan Shengde Electrical Machine Co., Ltd.	
Harbin Universe Photoelectron Co., Ltd.	
Fuan(Mindong) AnBo Electrical Machine Group	
Fuan Lixing Electrical Machine Co., Ltd.	X
Zhejiang Linan Jiapeng Metal Material Co., Ltd.	
Foshan Xinsheng Electrical Manufacturing Co., Ltd.	X
Kai Jili Group Co., Ltd.	
Yangzhou Shangbei Cable Electric Equipment Co., Ltd.	X
Fujian Tiangong Electrical Machine Co., Ltd.	X

(a) The above customers represented 28% and 11% of Lihua Electron's sales in 2011 and 2010, respectively. The coverage is lower for Lihua Electron sales because they have a high number of small volume customers. No customer accounted for more than 3% of Lihua Electron's sales in 2010. We selected the largest ten customers for confirmation.

We directly called each of the following customers of Lihua Copper:

Customer name	Verified Contact
Danyang Lihua Electron Co., Ltd. (b)	X
Zhangjiagang Union Copper Co., Ltd.	X
Shandong Hengbang Smelting Co., Ltd.	
Jinlong Copper Co., Ltd.	X
Jiangsu Jiangyang Cable Co., Ltd.	
Yixing Zhuzhu Cooper Co., Ltd.	
Jiangsu New Yuandong Cable Co., Ltd.	X
Wuxi Yuxin Cable Co., Ltd.	
Jiangsu Shangshang Cable Group Co., Ltd.	X
Yixing Yehong Trading Co., Ltd.	

(a) Represents intercompany transactions. We spoke with the contact person at Lihua Electron and also verified the sales to purchase accounting records of Lihua Electron
(b) The above customers represented 90% and 78% of Lihua Copper's sales in 2011 and 2010, respectively

In order to test the reasonableness of the Company's actual purchases as compared to their stated total capacity of 50,000 tons per year, we examined the Company's purchasing records for the year, which showed the following:

(Tons of copper purchased)	**Lihua Copper**	**Lihua Electron**	**Total**
Gross purchases	37,495	20,149	57,644
Less: intercompany purchases (Electron from Copper)	-	(13,650)	(13,650)
Net external purchases	37,495	6,499	43,994

Next, we reviewed the Company's 2010 Form 10-K and noted in "Item 6 – Selected Financial Data" the following disclosure regarding quantities of copper product shipped in 2010:

	Tons
CCA and copper wire	28,388
Copper anode	12,330
Refined copper rod	3,994
	44,712

The amount of copper purchased according to the Company's accounting records is reasonable compared with the reported amount of shipments. Next, we looked at the coverage that we achieved based on our supplier checks.

- For 2010, the suppliers that we spoke with accounted for 52% of net purchases from external suppliers, or approximately 23,000 tons of the approximately 44,000 tons purchased. Because we noted no exceptions in our testing, we did not expand our initial sample size. Of the remaining suppliers that we did not confirm, none accounted for more than 10% of total purchases.

- For first half of 2011, the suppliers that we spoke with accounted for 84% of net purchases from external suppliers, or approximately 25,500 tons of 30,500 tons purchased (the higher coverage in 2011 was due to the fact that one supplier accounted for approximately 31% of purchases in 2011, while none were higher than 13% in 2010). Of the remaining suppliers that we did not confirm, none accounted for more than 10% of total purchases.

Conclusion

Based on our discussions with the above customers and suppliers, we did not note any material exceptions. All of the customers and suppliers were aware of the Company, and verified that they did business with the Company. We asked each customer their opinion of the Company's products, and about timeliness of delivery and issuance of invoices. We did not receive any negative comments. We asked each supplier about the Company's reputation, and timeliness of payment. We did not receive any negative comments.

Additionally, we asked each customer/supplier to provide us with the amount of sales or purchases from their internal records. We then compared these sales and purchases to a list provided by the Company, and noted no material exceptions.

Finally, we independently verified, on a sample basis, that the contact names and phone numbers given to us by the Company were actual contact information for their customers and suppliers. We noted no exceptions.

Based on the coverage we achieved and the lack of any conflicting responses, the amount of the Company's purchases appear to be reasonably stated and in agreement with reported figures.

Internal Controls

Pursuant to the requirements of the Sarbanes Oxley Act of 2002 ("SOX"), the Company was required to report the specific findings of its internal control testing for its fiscal year ended December 31, 2010. As required, in its Form 10-K for the year ended December 31, 2010, the Company reported that, under the supervision of its principal executive officer and principal financial officer, it conducted an evaluation of the effectiveness of the design and operation of its disclosure controls and procedures. Based on this evaluation, the Company concluded as of December 31, 2010 that its disclosure controls and procedures were effective such that the material information required to be included in its SEC reports was recorded, processed, summarized and reported within the time periods specified in SEC rules. Using the Integrated Framework adopted by the Committee of Sponsoring Organizations of the Treadway Commission ("COSO"), management assessed the effectiveness of the Company's internal control over financial reporting, as of December 31, 2010, and determined it to be effective.

The conclusion that the Company's internal control over financial reporting was effective was based on comprehensive documentation, testing, remediation, and re-testing of the Company's internal controls in accordance with the COSO framework. Starting in early 2009, the Company underwent a comprehensive internal control review and reconstruction designed by Deloitte Consulting (Shanghai Office). This process included creating process narratives for key processes, risk evaluation of processes, and evaluation of entity level controls. Processes were then tested on a sample basis, with areas of significant deficiency or material weakness marked for remediation.

The Company tested and remediated three times between January 2009 and July 2010. During July 2010, testing determined that no material weaknesses in internal control over financial reporting existed. These processes were re-tested at December 31, 2010 and the same conclusion reached.

We examined the Company's SOX documentation, and also reviewed the critical internal control processes with the Company's financial staff. We noted the following:

- The Company uses Ufida financial software, and also uses Ufida's inventory-raw materials system. Ufida is a very common general ledger package used by Chinese companies.

- Since inventory is likely the most critical process, we operated the system in person and downloaded original inventory data for the period from January 2008 to June 2011, in order to test its accuracy compared to the financial reports. The data downloaded from the inventory system was basically consistent with the financial reports, with only immaterial differences.

- The inventory management system only included raw materials management, and did not include finished products management. Finished products are still accounted for using manual warehouse documentation.

- Raw materials data in the inventory management system is only updated once every 3-5 days, rather than on a real-time basis.

- After examining internal inventory documents, we found most are prepared manually, and even documents such as sales slips which are printed are not printed directly from the inventory management system.

- While the Company employs compensating controls to offset any variances, including physical inventory counts at each year-end, they would be better served by adding the finished goods module to their inventory tracking system, and making point of transaction entries into the system for all inventory movements, rather than inputting into the inventory system from manual documentation.

Generally speaking, the Company has done a better than average job of complying with its SOX requirements, as compared with other US-listed Chinese companies that we have reviewed. In many cases, companies will fabricate or severely under-document their SOX testing, and simply state that their controls are operating effectively without a solid basis for such conclusion. The Company took the prudent step of engaging an experienced SOX consultant two years before it was required to report on its controls. It has also maintained thorough documentation of its conclusion of control effectiveness, and would have an easily defensible position in the event the SEC, its auditors, or any other third party inquired about the basis for its position.

From a technical perspective, we noted that the Company did not follow the risk-based approach outlined by Auditing Standard No. 5, *An Audit of Internal Control Over Financial Reporting That Is Integrated with An Audit of Financial Statements*, ("AS-5") published by the Public Company Accounting Oversight Board ("PCAOB"). AS-5 calls for companies to identify all controls that affect financial reporting, and create a control matrix which contains a risk rating for each control, rating them high, medium or low. Testing is then performed based on the variable levels of risk, rather than testing every process. The Company took an all-encompassing approach of testing every control. The reason companies often choose this approach is to utilize the same testing framework used for the financial audit to test internal controls. This reduces the number of redundant test samples, as items tested in the financial audit can be used as evidence in the internal control test. This methodology can be flawed, however, because the risk based approach of AS-5 places more importance on testing high risk areas, and therefore results in larger sample sizes of high risk controls. Comprehensive testing results in more aggregate testing samples, but many of those samples are performed on low risk areas that would otherwise be scoped out using a risk based approach. While AS-5 does allow for samples from the financial audit to be used where testing overlaps, the financial audit and internal control testing were not meant to mirror each other.

Additionally, we noted that the Company's testing process is somewhat bottom-heavy, meaning that the Company performed a substantial amount of sample testing on individual processes but was less focused on entity level controls. Entity-Level Controls are internal controls that help ensure that management directives pertaining to the entire entity are carried out. AS-5 encourages a "top-down" approach, meaning that, because they are pervasive in nature, reliance can be placed on effective entity level controls, allowing companies to reduce control testing at the process level. If the Company's approach were more top heavy, they could eliminate some testing and focus the actual testing performed on higher-risk areas that are more likely to cause misstatements.

It is important to note that we did not re-test any or audit any specific processes or processes or controls. We reviewed the Company's documentation that they completed in connection with their SOX review, and analyzed their approach to the testwork in accordance with the COSO framework and AS-5. The Company is not required to have its SOX work papers audited for reporting purposes. The conclusion regarding the effectiveness of internal controls over financial reporting is that of management. Based on our review of the documentation, the design and testing of internal controls over financial reporting appears to have been performed within the COSO framework, and the conclusion of management appears to be reasonable based on the testing performed by the Company.

Copper Rod Smelter Down for Repair/Upgrade

During our site visit, we toured each of the Company's manufacturing facilities. We noted normal operations in the Lihua Electron facilities, but the production of copper rod was dormant.

We asked the Company to explain why this production line was not running, and their explanation was that the Company has two furnaces for producing copper rod and two furnaces for producing copper anode. Each furnace can be continuously used for 200 days and then requires a period of two months for overhauling and maintenance in order to remove magnesia crystal bricks and magnesia chrome bricks from the smelter. After continuous high-temperature production for about 200 days, these bricks can fall off, creating a safety hazard and influencing product quality. When one furnace is being overhauled, the other furnace related to that product remains in use.

During our initial visit in July 2011, we witnessed that one of two furnaces used in the production of copper anode was working normally, while the other was being repaired. However, we found both furnaces used for producing copper rod were both out of service. The Company said they were in process of dismantling one of the copper rod furnaces and installing a replacement. The process for replacement was as follows:

- The Company explained that they placed an order for the new furnace from an equipment supplier who began to deliver the new furnace accessories to the Company starting in December 2010.

- The furnace was assembled offsite between December 2010 and May 2011, to allow for continued usage of the existing furnaces. Normal assembly for this type of furnace is approximately 3-4 months. The Company explained that their process was slightly longer due to the Chinese holiday, which shut down assembly for more than a month.

- In May 2011, installation of the new furnace into the workshop was commenced. At that time, production of the original two copper rod furnaces was stopped, since the installation could not be completed for safety reasons while the original furnaces were running.

- At the beginning of June 2011, after the initial installation was completed, the original copper rod furnace still in place resumed production for four weeks.

- Upon installation, the Company learned that the new furnace's smoke venting pipelines were inconsistent with those of the original furnace, so modification was required. The two furnaces' smoke venting pipelines are connected, so all copper rod production had to be stopped while the smoke venting pipelines were re-outfitted. This stoppage began at the end of June 2011 and is expected to be completed in August 2011.

- We noted accessories to be installed on the new furnace and took photographs.

During our return visit in August 2011, we noted that the original copper rod furnace (the one not being replaced) had resumed production.

Because copper rod is the main raw material of copper wire, another of the Company's products, we asked the Company how the production stoppage of copper rod would influence the production of copper wire. The Company's response was that they were using existing inventory on hand to fill orders for copper wire. We counted the stored copper rod in the Company's warehouse and estimated they had about 600 tons on hand. According to the Company's production volume, the copper rod in stock equates to about two weeks wroth of copper wire production. The Company informed us that, in the event their current stock was exhausted, they would temporarily purchase copper rod in the open market for short term production purposes.

Moreover, the Company told us that Bin Yang from Roth Capital had visited the Company with other investors in April 2011 and had witnessed the production of copper rod when all furnaces were active. We contacted Bin Yang and were sent photographs of the operational copper rod furnaces, as well as confirmation from Bin Yang that the furnaces were operational during the visit.

We also checked the relevant financial records and contracts with respect to the furnace renovation project. The total contract amount of this project is RMB 4.2 million (about $640,000), of which RMB 1.2 million (about $180,000) has been paid. We reviewed the contract and related payment documentation.

Based on our observations, discussions with the Company, and review of project documentation, it spears reasonable that the copper rod furnace was inactive for the reasons described above.

New Copper Facility

The Company is currently constructing a new facility to increase its production capacity, as its sales of copper anode are currently capacity-constrained.

The Company received a document entitled, "Reply on approving a new construction project production line with the annual production of 170,000-ton recycled copper and copper anode" issued by the Danyang Development and Reform Commission on August 11, 2010. This document represents approval to build the new facility.

The construction currently in process relates to the Phase I addition of 50,000 tons of capacity through the purchase and installation of two copper anode production lines. The fixed assets investment during Phase I is approximately $40 million, comprised of approximately $10 million of land costs (including approximately $5 million for the land acquisition and approximately $5 million in costs borne by the Company for integration work such as road construction, tree and crop replacement, and restitution to the local village), $10-12 million in infrastructure and physical plant costs (including site preparation, plant construction, and water and drainage system construction) and $18-20 million in production equipment (each 25,000 smelter costing approximately $9-10 million including the smelter itself, plus water treatment, water circulation, and environmental protection facilities).

To date, the Company has paid approximately $10 million (RMB 66,200,840) for the land purchase and relocations costs. We traced the payment details comprising this entire amount to bank statements provided by the Company. We did not obtain the bank statements independently, as the cash verification process was outside of the scope of this report (see section entitled "Cash Verification"). We also reviewed the land purchase agreement and noted that the amounts agreed to the costs described above. The Company has not yet received the land use certificate from the government, but expects to receive it during August 2011.

The Company will also require additional working capital of approximately $100 million. The Company explained that this working capital requirement is based on the condition that all raw materials are imported from the US. There are several reasons why it is advantageous for the Company to import raw materials from the US:

1. The quality of raw material in the US is better than in China. In fact, the raw materials of most suppliers of scrap copper in China are imported from the US
2. The Company needs stable and large-scale suppliers after its expansion. Chinese raw material suppliers are unreliable, and in fact they import most of their materials from the US, so the Company is better served sourcing directly from the supplier.
3. The Company can save approximately $100-150 per ton if purchased directly from the US supplier.

The Company previously has not imported directly because it did not have an import license. The Company received its "Registration license for domestic consignees of imported solid waste as raw materials" from the General Administration of Quality Supervision, Inspection and Quarantine. The license was issued on November 23, 2010 and is valid through November 22, 2013.

The disadvantage of direct sourcing is that raw materials sourced in the US require three months from placement of the order to delivery, consisting of: three weeks for preparing the goods by the supplier, seven weeks for marine delivery, and three weeks for PRC customs formalities and delivery.

The Company plans to access the $100 million working capital requirement through a credit line with a PRC bank. The Company is applying for credit lines with Industrial and Commercial Bank of

China, China Construction Bank, China Merchants Bank, Jiangsu Bank, and Nanjing Bank. No definitive agreements have been signed to date for the funding.

The Company is in the negotiation stages with US-based suppliers and has not yet signed any definitive supply agreements. If a long-term cooperation is established with a US-based supplier, the Company expects that the supplier will be able to shorten the goods preparation time, reducing the amount of working capital required.

Danyang Huaying Resource Recycling, Ltd.

Danyang Huaying Resource Recycling, Ltd. ("Huaying") is a scrap metal reseller with registered capital of RMB 41.5 million, which was contributed by:

- Wang Yaying, Lihua International's COO, Secretary and Director (RMB 33.2 million),
- Wang Liying (RMB 4.15 million), sister of Wang Yaying and sister-in-law of Lihua International's CEO and Chairman Zhu Jianhua, and also legal representative and general manager of Huaying
- Zhu Junying (RMB 4.15 million)

Huaying's registered address is the same address as that of Lihua Copper and Lihua Electron. Based on the ownership by related parties and the fact that the registered address is the same as Lihua Copper and Lihua Electron, we investigated whether Huaying is an undisclosed related party.

Pursuant to Item 404 of Regulation S-K, public companies (registrants) are required to disclose, "any transaction, since the beginning of the registrant's last fiscal year, or any currently proposed transaction, in which the registrant was or is to be a participant and the amount involved exceeds $120,000, and in which any related person had or will have a direct or indirect material interest." Lihua International did not disclose any business dealings with Huaying in its related party transactions in its SEC filings.

We independently obtained the SAIC reports of Huaying for 2009 and 2010 from the Danyang SAIC office and confirmed the ownership and management information above. We then spoke with Huaying's financial manager and she told us that Huaying operated its business out of a sales office in Guangdong. Huaying did not have any production facilities, they were simply a broker of scrap metal. The registered address is the same as that of Lihua Copper and Lihua Electron because the Guangdong office was not open when Huaying received its initial registered capital infusion in June 2008, so they used Lihua's address for convenience due to Wang Liying's relationship with Wang Yaying and Zhu Jianhua. The address was never updated. Wang Liying has acted as Huaying's general manager since inception.

During 2010, Huaying reported in its SAIC filings sales of RMB 41.4 million (about $6.3 million) and a net loss of RMB 11.7 million (about $1.8 million). The financial manager explained that in 2010, Huaying was inefficient and unable to make profits on the resale of scrap iron, aluminum, and copper, and scaled back its workforce. Then in 2011, they shut down their office and discontinued their business to avoid incurring further losses. The financial manager stated that Huaying had never done any business with Lihua International, Lihua Copper, or Lihua Electron. The SAIC reports also confirmed that Huaying had no fixed assets as of December 31, 2010.

We further reviewed the Company's purchase records, and confirmed that no purchases were made from Huaying in 2009, 2010, or 2011. While such purchases could be included under a false supplier name in the Company's records (to exceed $120,000 in purchases from Huaying, the Company would only need to purchase about 15 of the 43,995 tons purchased in 2010), we did independently verify a substantial portion of the Company's copper purchases (see section entitled "Channel Checks" for description of procedures and findings) without exception. While this is not conclusive evidence that there is no relationship with Huaying, it does provide circumstantial support. Since access to Huaying's financial data and source documents was outside the scope of our investigation, this is the extent of procedures we were able to perform.

If purchases made by the Company from Huaying were less than $120,000 in any given fiscal year, the Company is not required to disclose Huaying as a related party, despite the ownership by Company management and their relatives. The Company should request that Huaying immediately change its registered address to reflect its actual place of business.

Documents Reviewed

Following is a comprehensive list of source documents obtained from the Company and other sources that we reviewed in connection with this report.

1. The Company's basic information

- 1.1. Lihua Copper
  - 1.1.1. Original and one copy of business license of Jiangsu Lihua Copper Co., Ltd. (registered capital of $65 million, paid-up capital of $46 million, annual examination of 2010)
  - 1.1.2. Original and one copy of organization code certificate (annual examination of 2010)
  - 1.1.3. Original and one copy of tax registration certificate
  - 1.1.4. Articles of association (registered capital of $15 million on March 15, 2009)
  - 1.1.5. Copy of capital verification report on April 26, 2010, with registered capital of $65 million and paid-up capital of $31 million

- 1.1.6. Copper import registration certificate (General Administration of Quality Supervision, from November 23, 2010 to November 22, 2013)
- 1.1.7. The annual examination report of industrial and commercial bureau

1.2. Lihua Electron

- 1.2.1. Original and one copy of business license of Jiangsu Lihua Electron Co., Ltd. (registered capital of $10.5 million and paid-up capital of $10.5 million, annual examination of 2010)
- 1.2.2. Copy of the production license for industrial products of Danyang Lihua electron Co., Ltd. (from January 15, 2009 to January 14, 2014)
- 1.2.3. Original and one copy of organization code certificate (annual examination of 2011)
- 1.2.4. Original and one copy of tax registration certificate
- 1.2.5. Articles of association (registered capital of $2.2 million on March 15, 2009)
- 1.2.6. Copy of capital verification report on January 21, 2010, with registered capital of $10.5 million
- 1.2.7. The annual examination report of industrial and commercial bureau

2. Government documents

2.1. Lihua Copper

- 2.1.1. The copy of Notice of Approval of New Construction Project of 60,000-ton non-ferrous metals (refined copper rod and oxygen-free copper rod), bimetal materials (special electromagnetic wire) by Development and Reform Commission of Danyang (total investment of $29 million and the issuance date is July 23, 2008)
- 2.1.2. The copy of Reply on approving a new construction project production line with the annual production of

170,000-ton recycled copper and copper anode issued by Development and Reform Commission of Danyang (total investment of $99.98 million and the issuance date is August 11, 2010)

2.1.3. Examination and opinion on the Environmental Impact Statement for the production project with an annual capacity of 170,000-ton recycled copper and copper anode plate of Jiangsu Lihua Copper Co., Ltd. (Environment Protection Bureau on August 2, 2010)

2.1.4. Preliminary examining opinions on the land used for the project with an annual capacity of 170,000-ton recycled copper anode plate of Jiangsu Lihua Copper Co., Ltd. (Land and Resources Bureau on July 23, 2010)

2.2.Lihua Electron

2.2.1. The copy of Notice on approving a capital increase project of annual production of 6,000-ton copper clad special electromagnetic wire by Development and Reform Commission of Danyang (capital increase of $2.8 million and the issuance date is June 10, 2007)

2.2.2.Approval for environmental evaluation

3. Production documents

3.1. Lihua Copper

3.1.1. Details of major products

3.1.2. Chart of production process of refined copper rod

3.1.3. Chart of production process of anode plate

3.1.4. Patent certificate (oxygen-free copper rod air pressure taking-up device, March 4, 2009)

3.1.5. Trademark registration certificate (Meilihua, from August 21, 2010 to August 20, 2020)

3.1.6. Reconstruction contract of shaft furnace (December 31, 2010)

3.1.7. Payment document for 170,000-ton new project and purchase agreement of 180 mu land

3.2. Lihua Electron

3.2.1. Details of major products

3.2.2. Chart of production of enameled wire

3.2.3. Patent certificate (CCA enameled wire and production process, December 8, 2010)

4. Suppliers

4.1. Lihua Copper

4.1.1. Contact information of major suppliers

4.1.2. Supply of materials over the years of major suppliers

4.2. Lihua Electron

4.2.1. List of top customers

4.2.2. Supply of materials over the years of major suppliers

5. Customers

5.1. Lihua Copper

5.1.1. Copies of material purchase and sales contracts

5.1.2. Sales in the past 12 months of the top 10 customers

5.1.3. Contact information of the top 10 customers

5.2. Lihua Electron

5.2.1. Copies of material purchase and sales contracts

5.2.2. Purchases in the past 12 months of the top 10 customers

5.2.3. Contact information of the top 10 customers

6. Asset certificates

6.1. Lihua Copper

6.1.1. Copy of property ownership certificate (16950.86 square meters on March 12, 2009)

6.1.2. Copy of property ownership certificate (4738.18 square meters on March 12, 2009)

6.1.3. Copy of property ownership certificate (207.26 square meters on March 12, 2009)

6.1.4. Copy of property ownership certificate (11058.07 square meters on March 12, 2009)

6.1.5. Copy of land certificate (33332.0 square meters in Jide and Wuxing villages, Houxiang Township of Danyang from June 6, 2008 to March 32, 2058)

6.1.6. Copy of land certificate (33333.7 square meters in Houxiang Township of Danyang from October 6, 2008 to October 6, 2058)

6.2. Lihua Electron

6.2.1. Copy of property ownership certificate (4121.54 square meters on June 5, 2008)

6.2.2. Copy of property ownership certificate (4703.27 square meters on June 5, 2008)

6.2.3. Copy of land certificate (10470.8 square meters in Wuxing village, Houxiang Township of Danyang from October 6, 2008 to October 5, 2058)

7. Internal control documents

7.1. Organization chart of Lihua International (Lihua Electron Lihua Copper)

7.2. List of middle-level management persons

7.3. Management regulations (including purchasing payment process, inventory management and cost accounting, personnel and salary management, fixed asset management, income and receipt management, fund management, financial reports and financial closing, taxation management, and option management)

7.4. Information of all office sites and office leasing contracts

7.5. Payroll form and social insurance details of December, 2009, December, 2010, May or June, 2011

7.6. Transceiver internal control documents of inventory

8. Financial information

8.1. Lihua Copper

8.1.1. Lihua Copper's financial information for 2009 (including financial statements, TB, inventory, income, cost, AR, AP, other AP, prepayment, fixed assets, and gross profit)

8.1.2. Lihua Copper's financial information for 2010 (including financial statements, TB, inventory, income, cost, AR, AP, other AP, prepayment, fixed assets, and gross profit)

8.1.3. Lihua Copper's financial information for Jan.-June 2011 (including financial statements, TB, inventory, income, cost, AR, AP, other AP, prepayment, fixed assets, and gross profit)

8.1.4. Lihua Copper's list of computer system raw material in, out and inventory from 2009 to June 2011

8.1.5. Lihua Copper's VAT return of December, 2010 and January-June, 2011

8.1.6. Tax return of VAT and income tax from 2009 to June 2011

8.1.7. Cost statement by products income from year 2008 to June 2011

8.1.8. Details of deposit in Agricultural Bank of China from year 2010 to June 2011

8.1.9. Lihua Copper's financial information for 2008

8.2. Lihau Electron

8.2.1. Lihua Electron's financial information for 2009 (including financial statements, TB, inventory, income, cost, AR, AP, other AP, prepayment, fixed assets, and gross profit)

8.2.2. Lihua Electron's financial information for 2010 (including financial statements, TB, inventory, income, cost, AR, AP, other AP, prepayment, fixed assets, and gross profit)

8.2.3. Lihua Electron's financial information for Jan.-June 2011 (including financial statements, TB, inventory, income, cost, AR, AP, other AP, prepayment, fixed assets, and gross profit)

8.2.4. Copy of Loan Agreement from Agricultural Bank of China ($15 million, from April 21, 2011 to April 20, 2012)

8.2.5. Copy of Collateral Agreement for $15 million from Agricultural Bank of China (warrantor: Danyang Tianyi Communications Co., Ltd.)

8.2.6. Lihua Electron's computer system raw material in, out and inventory from 2008 to June 2011

8.2.7. Lihua Electron's VAT return of December, 2010 and January- June, 2011

8.2.8. Tax return of VAT and income tax from 2009 to June 2011

8.2.9. Lihua Electron's financial information for 2008

8.2.10. Tax return of VAT and income tax for 2008

8.2.11. Cost statement by products income from year 2008 to June 2011

8.2.12. Certificate of paying VAT and income tax for 2010

8.2.13. Details of deposit in Agricultural Bank of China from year 2010 to June 2011

8.2.14. Approval documents for preferential tax in the previous years

9. Audit data and post processing data

9.1. Audit consolidation table for 2008

9.2. Audit consolidation table for 2009

9.3. Audit consolidation table for 2010

9.4. Reconciliation among financial book data, audit data, data in SAT, and data in SAIC

Biographies

Author: David A. Dodge

David A. Dodge has been an independent financial consultant since 2007, acting as interim CFO and/or providing accounting, management, and financial reporting services for Anhui Taiyang Poultry Co., Inc. (OTCBB:DUKS), TTC Technology Corp (formerly SmarTire Systems, Inc., TCLIF.PK), Futuremedia PLC (FMDAY.PK), and multiple privately held Chinese companies in the process of going public and raising capital in North America. Mr. Dodge has also authored a number of due diligence reports on Chinese companies, both public and private. Previously, Mr. Dodge served as CFO of NeoMedia Technologies, Inc. (OTCBB: NEOM), a U.S. public company, from 2002 through 2007. From 1999 to 2002, Mr. Dodge held various finance-related positions with NeoMedia, including Director of Financial Reporting, Director of Financial Planning, and Controller. Prior to his public company experience, Mr. Dodge was an auditor with Ernst & Young LLP from 1997 to 1999. Mr. Dodge holds a B.A. in economics from Yale University and an M.S. in accounting from the University of Hartford, and is also a Certified Public Accountant (inactive).

Fieldwork: Yang Hao

Yang Hao, graduated from the Renmin University of China School of Business with an MA Degree in Accounting. He has served as capital manager, audit manager and accounting manager for large state-owned enterprises, a Hong Kong-listed company, and a U.S. publicly listed company where he assisted in the reverse merger and funding processes. He has also held the position of finance manager with the U.S. public company. Mr. Yang is familiar with both Chinese and American accounting standards, including GAAP. In his various positions he has been responsible for establishing corporate internal controls, corporate funds management and financial control systems, along with the budget management system. Mr. Yang currently serves as a consultant to both American and Chinese companies in the fields of corporate audit, business, management and financial processes and controls.

EXHIBIT A

Biographies

Fieldwork: Chang Yanfeng

Chang Yanfeng graduated from Renmin University of China with a BA Degree in Accounting. He has served as Audit Specialist and Accounting Manager at the headquarters of the China Printing Group; Finance Vice Manager and Settlement Supervisor for Dalian Gome Co., Ltd; Vice Manager of the Financial Center Settlement Management Department at Gome's (a Hong Kong-listed company) world headquarters; and in a U.S. publicly listed company where he assisted in the reverse merger and funding processes. Mr. Chang is familiar with both Chinese and American accounting policies and procedures and is an expert in ERP systems management. Mr. Chang currently serves as a consultant to both American and Chinese companies in the fields of corporate audit, financial processes and ERP systems analysis.

Internal Controls Expert: David S. Lethem

David S. Lethem is currently serving as an SEC/Audit Consultant for public companies, most recently NeoMedia Technologies, Inc (OTCBB:NEOM) and NeoGenomics, Inc. (OTCBB:NGNM). From 2005 through 2007, Mr. Lethem served as Director of Internal Audit for NeoMedia. Prior to NeoMedia, he served as Internal Audit Manager for a public company, Source Interlink (NASDAQ:SORC), and has served as a consultant for Sarbanes Oxley and SEC compliance with Accume Partners. Prior to his public company experience, Mr. Lethem served as Chief Financial Officer of two community banks, and has also served as controller for two private companies. Mr. Lethem holds a B.A in History from the University of Dubuque and an MBA from California Coast University, and is also a Certified Internal Auditor.

EXHIBIT B
List of Industrial Products

Exhibit B

Search

* Home * Favorites * internal mail

Home | Quality and Technical Supervision Information | Law Centre | Jeng Min interactive | Site Map | Enquiry Service

Current position: Industrial Production License >> application card catalog

Industrial products production license directory

[Print] [Close]

No.	Product category	Name of the corresponding implementation details	Rules of order number	Approved Category	Number	Implementation time
1	Wood-based panels	Wood-based panels	1	Provincial Certification	(X) XK03-002	January 19, 2011
2	Construction steel	Reinforced concrete with hot-rolled ribbed steel bars	2	Administration Certification	XK05-001	March 1, 2011
		Cold-rolled ribbed steel bars	3	Administration Certification	XK05-002	March 1, 2011
3	Prestressed concrete steel	Prestressed concrete steel	4	Administration Certification	XK05-003	March 1, 2011
4	Refractory	Refractory	5	Provincial Certification	(X) XK05-004	January 19, 2011
5	Wire rope	Wire rope	6	Administration Certification	XK05-005	March 1, 2011
6	Bearing steel	Bearing steel	7	Administration Certification	XK05-006	March 1, 2011
7	Pump	Pump	8	Provincial Certification	(X) XK06-005	January 19, 2011
8	Air Compressors	Air Compressors	9	Administration Certification	XK06-010	March 1, 2011
9	Battery	Lead-acid batteries	10	Administration Certification	XK06-006	March 1, 2011
10	Mobile thresher	Mobile thresher	11	Administration Certification	XK06-012	March 1, 2011
11	Explosion-proof electrical	Explosion-proof electrical	12	Administration Certification	XK06-014	March 1, 2011
12	Grinding wheel	Grinding wheel	13	Administration Certification	XK06-011	March 1, 2011
13	Internal combustion engine	Internal combustion engine	14	Administration Certification	XK06-002	March 1, 2011
14	Wire & Cable	Wire & Cable	15	Provincial Certification	(X) XK06-001	January 19, 2011
15	Welding	Welding	16	Provincial Certification	(X) XK06-009	January 19, 2011
16	Power Rectifier	Power Rectifiers (Power Electronics) products	17	Administration Certification	XK06-008	March 1, 2011
17	Small light lifting and transport equipment	Small light lifting and transport equipment	18	Administration Certification	XK06-003	March 1, 2011
		Scheduling winch	19	Administration Certification	XK06-004	March 1, 2011
		Satellite television ground	20	Administration	XK09-002	March 1, 2011

* Open Government Information Catalog
* Government Information Guide
* Annual Report on Open Government Information
* apply for an open application process by
* monitoring of complaints

EXHIBIT B
List of Industrial Products

No.	Product	Product unit	No.	Certification	License No.	Date
	Satellite television	receiving equipment		Certification		
18	ground receiving equipment	Dedicated satellite television broadcast satellite ground receiving equipment	21	Administration Certification	XK09-005	March 1, 2011
19	IC card and IC card reader machine	IC card and IC card reader machine	22	Administration Certification	XK09-008	March 1, 2011
20	Fertilizer	Fertilizer	23	Provincial Certification	(X) XK13-001	January 19, 2011
		Phosphate	24	Provincial Certification	(X) XK13-002	January 19, 2011
21	Pesticide	Pesticide	25	Administration Certification	XK13-005	March 1, 2011
22	Rubber Products	Rubber hoses and hose assemblies	26	Provincial Certification	(X) XK13-022	January 19, 2011
		Flame-retardant conveyor belt	27	Provincial Certification	(X) XK13-023	January 19, 2011
		Automotive V-belt	28	Provincial Certification	(X) XK13-028	January 19, 2011
		Rubber sealing products	29	Provincial Certification	(X) XK13-025	January 19, 2011
23	BOP and BOP control unit	BOP and BOP control unit	30	Administration Certification	XK14-001	March 1, 2011
24	Drilling tool suspension	Drilling tool suspension	31	Administration Certification	XK14-002	March 1, 2011
25	Electric Blanket	Electric blanket	32	Provincial Certification	(X) XK16-001	January 19, 2011
26	Bicycle	Bicycle	33	Provincial Certification	(X) XK16-002	January 19, 2011
27	Glasses	Glasses	34	Administration Certification	XK16-003	March 1, 2011
		Fitting glasses	35	Provincial Certification	(X) XK16-005	January 19, 2011
28	Prestressed concrete sleeper	Prestressed concrete sleeper	36	Administration Certification	XK17-002	March 1, 2011
29	Prestressed concrete simple beam bridge	Prestressed concrete simple beam bridge	37	Administration Certification	XK17-004	March 1, 2011
30	Port Handling Equipment	Port Handling Equipment	38	Administration Certification	XK18-002	March 1, 2011
31	Highway bridge bearings	Highway bridge bearings	39	Administration Certification	XK18-004	March 1, 2011
32	Brake fluid	Motor vehicle brake fluid	40	Provincial Certification	(X) XK18-001	January 19, 2011
33	Special labor protection articles	Special labor protection articles	41	Provincial Certification	(X) XK22-001	January 19, 2011
34	Construction steel scaffolding fasteners	Construction steel scaffolding fasteners	42	Provincial Certification	(X) XK23-001	January 19, 2011
35	Construction hoist	Construction hoist	43	Administration Certification	XK21-004	March 1, 2011
36	Motorcycle helmets	Motorcycle helmets	44	Provincial Certification	(X) XK15-001	January 19, 2011
37	Cement	Cement	45	Administration Certification	XK08-001	March 1, 2011
38	Pipes	Pipes	46	Provincial Certification	(X) XK08-002	January 19, 2011
39	Friction materials and sealing products	Mechanical seal	47	Administration Certification	XK06-007	March 1, 2011
		Friction materials	48	Administration Certification	XK06-003	March 1, 2011
		Non-metallic sealing products	49	Administration Certification	XK06-004	March 1, 2011
				Provincial	(X)	

EXHIBIT B
List of Industrial Products

40	Waterproof membrane	Waterproof membrane	50	Provincial Certification	(X) XK08-005	January 19, 2011
41	Copper and copper alloy tubes	Copper and copper alloy tubes	51	Administration Certification	XK20-001	March 1, 2011
42	Aluminum, titanium processed products	Aluminum Profiles	52	Administration Certification	XK20-002	March 1, 2011
		Titanium and titanium alloy products	53	Administration Certification	XK10-003	March 1, 2011
43	Radio communications tower and mast	Radio communications tower and mast	54	Administration Certification	XK11-001	March 1, 2011
44	Electrical fittings	Electrical fittings	55	Administration Certification	XK04-001	March 1, 2011
45	Transmission line tower	Transmission line tower	56	Administration Certification	XK04-002	March 1, 2011
46	Power dispatch communications equipment	Power line carrier communication products	57	Administration Certification	XK04-003	March 1, 2011
		Power Line traps and filters with	58	Administration Certification	XK04-004	March 1, 2011
47	Hydraulic metal structures	Hydraulic metal structures	59	Administration Certification	XK07-001	March 1, 2011
48	Hydrological Instruments	Hydrological Instruments	60	Provincial Certification	(X) XK07-002	January 19, 2011
49	Geotechnical Instruments	Geotechnical Instruments	61	Provincial Certification	(X) XK07-005	January 19, 2011
50	Refrigeration Equipment	Refrigeration Equipment	62	Administration Certification	XK06-015	March 1, 2011
51	Life-saving equipment	Life jacket	63	Administration Certification	XK18-005	March 1, 2011
52	Pumping equipment	Pumping	64	Administration Certification	XK14-005	March 1, 2011
		Rod and Coupling	65	Administration Certification	XK14-004	March 1, 2011
		Pump	66	Administration Certification	XK14-005	March 1, 2011
53	Gas appliances	Gas water heater	67	Administration Certification	XK23-005	March 1, 2011
		Gas Regulator (box)	68	Administration Certification	XK23-006	March 1, 2011
		Gas stove	69	Administration Certification	XK23-007	March 1, 2011
54	Food grinding machine	Food grinding machine	70	Administration Certification	XK06-013	March 1, 2011
55	Instrument to identify counterfeit RMB	Instrument to identify counterfeit RMB	71	Administration Certification	XK09-001	July 4, 2011
		Chemical reagents	72	Provincial Certification	(X) XK13-011	January 19, 2011
		Acetylene	73	Provincial Certification	(X) XK13-005	January 19, 2011
		Compressed, liquefied gas	74	Provincial Certification	(X) XK13-010	January 19, 2011
		Class I inorganic hazardous chemicals	75	Provincial Certification	(X) XK13-006	January 19, 2011
		Class II inorganic hazardous chemicals	76	Provincial Certification	(X) XK13-006	January 19, 2011
		Inorganic products of dangerous chemicals (III type)	77	Provincial Certification	(X) XK13-006	January 19, 2011
		Chlor-alkali	78	Provincial Certification	(X) XK13-008	January 19, 2011
		Industrial nitrate	79	Provincial Certification	(X) XK15-009	January 19, 2011

EXHIBIT B
List of Industrial Products

56 Dangerous chemicals	Dye intermediates	80	Provincial Certification	(X) XK13-[illegible]	January 19, 2011
	Sulfuric acid	81	Provincial Certification	(X) XK13-[illegible]	January 19, 2011
	Cell nitrocellulose	82	Provincial Certification	(X) XK13-[illegible]	January 19, 2011
	Liquid anhydrous ammonia, sodium cyanide	83	Provincial Certification	(X) XK13-[illegible]	January 19, 2011
	Hazardous organic chemicals class 3	84	Provincial Certification	(X) XK13-[illegible]	January 19, 2011
	Hazardous organic chemicals, Class 8	85	Provincial Certification	(X) XK13-[illegible]	January 19, 2011
	Calcium carbide (calcium carbide)	86	Provincial Certification	(X) XK13-[illegible]	January 19, 2011
	Paint	87	Provincial Certification	(X) XK13-[illegible]	January 19, 2011
	Fireworks with hazardous chemicals	88	Provincial Certification	(X) XK13-[illegible]	January 19, 2011
	Ink	89	Provincial Certification	(X) XK13-[illegible]	January 19, 2011
	Oil	90	Provincial Certification	(X) XK13-[illegible]	January 19, 2011
	Adhesive	91	Provincial Certification	(X) XK13-[illegible]	January 19, 2011
	Synthetic resin	92	Provincial Certification	(X) XK13-[illegible]	January 19, 2011
	Ferrosilicon	93	Provincial Certification	(X) XK13-[illegible]	January 19, 2011
57 Dangerous chemicals, packaging materials and containers	Dangerous chemicals, packaging materials and containers	94	Provincial Certification	(X) XK12-001	January 19, 2011
58 Cotton processing machinery	Cotton processing machinery	95	Administration Certification	XK[illegible]-001	March 1, 2011
59 Anti-counterfeit technology products	Anti-counterfeit labels	96	Administration Certification	XK19-[illegible]	March 1, 2011
	Security tickets	97	Administration Certification	XK19-[illegible]	March 1, 2011
	Anti-counterfeit material	98	Administration Certification	XK19-002	March 1, 2011
60 Wireless radio and television transmitting equipment	Wireless radio and television transmitting equipment	99	Administration Certification	XK[illegible]	March 1, 2011
61 Fiscal Cash Register	Fiscal Cash Register	100	Administration Certification	XK[illegible]	March 1, 2011
	Financial Tax Control Cash Register	101	Administration Certification	XK[illegible]	March 1, 2011

Site Policy | Site Map | Contact Us

Address: North Road Yuhui, Chaoyang District, No. 3, ICP record number: Beijing ICP No. [illegible]

EXHIBIT C-1

Reconciliations between Tax Reports and Management Accounts

Lihua Electron - 2008
All amounts in RMB
Debit (credit)

BALANCE SHEET

	Management Accounts	VAT Return	SAT Return	SAIC Return	Variance: Management accounts vs. VAT Return	Variance: Management accounts vs. SAT Return	Variance: Management accounts vs. SAIC Return	Variance: SAT vs. SAIC
Current Assets								
Cash and cash equivalents	165,828,991			165,828,991			0.00%	
Account Receivable	34,465,104			34,465,104				
Notes receivables	2,200,000			2,200,000				
Other Receivables				6,311,384				
Inventory	4,011,488			4,011,488				
Intercompany	5,369,715							
Total current assets	211,875,298	-	-	212,816,967				
Non-current assets								
Net of PPE	50,855,875			58,855,875				
Intangible Assets	7,656,388			7,721,804				
Total Assets	270,387,561	-	-	271,394,646			0.37%	
Current Liabilities								
Account payable	(11,040,658)			(11,040,658)				
Other payables	(2,840,407)			(674,819)				
Income tax payable	(2,743,654)							
Tax payables	(2,269,446)			(4,920,317)				
Other tax payables	(21,181)			(21,181)				
Short - term loans	(42,000,000)			(42,000,000)				
Total current liabilities	(60,915,346)	-	-	(58,656,975)				
Shareholders' Equity								
Common stock -par value	(16,738,686)			(16,738,686)				
Additional paid in capital	(822,149)			(822,149)				
Retained earnings	(172,720,242)			(185,457,179)				
PRC statutory reserve	(19,191,138)			(9,719,657)				
Total shareholder's equity	(209,472,215)	-	-	(212,737,671)				
Total equity and liabilities	(270,387,561)	-	-	(271,394,646)				
	-	-	-	-				

INCOME STATEMENT

	Management Account	VAT Return	SAT Return	SAIC Return	Variance: Management accounts vs. VAT Return	Variance: Management accounts vs. SAT Return	Variance: Management accounts vs. SAIC Return	Variance: SAT vs. SAIC
Revenue	(347,302,069)	(344,216,846)	(347,327,508)	(347,302,069)	-0.89%	0.01%	0.00%	0.01%
Cost of Good Sold	230,366,709		230,366,709	230,366,709		0.00%	0.00%	0.00%
Sales tax and surcharges	230,215			230,215				
Gross Profit	(116,705,145)		(116,960,799)	(116,705,145)		0.22%	0.00%	0.22%
Other (income) expenses	(25,885)		16,077,418	(25,985)				
Selling expenses	4,861,839			5,103,569				
Administration expenses	8,604,469			6,744,021				
Finance costs	3,137,535			3,482,306				
Other Expenses				517,853				
Net (income) from operation	(100,127,287)		(100,883,381)	(100,883,381)		0.76%	0.76%	0.00%
Income tax	12,610,423		12,610,423	12,648,852				
Net (Income)/Loss	(87,516,864)		(88,272,958)	(88,234,529)		0.86%	0.82%	0.04%

Note 1: VAT returns do not include any financial information other than sales
Note 2: SAT returns do not include balance sheet information

EXHIBIT C-2

Reconciliations between Tax Reports and Management Accounts

Lihua Electron - 2009
All amounts in RMB
Debit (credit)

BALANCE SHEET	Management Accounts	VAT Return	SAT Return	SAIC Return	Variance: Management accounts vs. VAT Return	Variance: Management accounts vs. SAT Return	Variance: Management accounts vs. SAIC Return	Variance: SAT vs. SAIC
Current Assets								
Cash and cash equivalents	208,856,854			208,656,854			0.00%	
Account Receivable	59,505,507			59,505,507				
Other Receivables				61,929,715				
Prepayment to suppliers				15,900				
Inventory	46,029,442			46,029,442				
Intercompany	61,869,715							
Total current assets	376,061,518	-	-	376,137,418				
Non-current assets								
Net of PPE	54,676,418			54,676,418				
Intangible Assets	7,489,791			7,489,791				
Deposit for fixed assets	15,900							
Total Assets	438,243,627	-	-	438,303,627			0.01%	
Current Liabilities								
Account payable	(10,346,400)			(10,346,401)				
Other payables	(3,164,213)			(11,075,378)				
Income tax payable	(6,246,849)							
Tax payables	(1,226,899)			(7,535,905)				
Intercompany	(7,855,845)							
Other tax payables	(10,957)							
Accrued expenses	(22,125)			(22,125)				
Short - term loans	(15,000,000)			(15,000,000)				
Total current liabilities	(43,873,288)	-	-	(43,979,809)				
Shareholders' Equity								
Common stock -par value	(57,653,582)			(57,712,086)				
Additional paid in capital	(828,978)			(828,978)				
Retained earnings	(302,299,001)			(306,891,616)				
PRC statutory reserve	(33,588,778)			(28,891,138)				
Total shareholder's equity	(394,370,339)	-	-	(394,323,818)				
Total equity and liabilities	(438,243,627)	-	-	(438,303,627)			0.01%	
	-	-	-	-				

INCOME STATEMENT	Management Account	VAT Return	SAT Return	SAIC Return	Variance: Management accounts vs. VAT Return	Variance: Management accounts vs. SAT Return	Variance: Management accounts vs. SAIC Return	Variance: SAT vs. SAIC
Revenue	(747,298,761)	(747,298,761)	(747,298,761)	(747,298,761)	0.00%	0.00%	0.00%	0.00%
Cost of Good Sold	566,929,378		566,929,378	566,929,378		0.00%	0.00%	0.00%
Sales tax and surcharges	231,834		231,834	231,834				
Gross Profit	(180,135,549)		(180,135,549)	(180,135,549)		0.00%	0.00%	0.00%
Selling expenses	8,309,966		8,309,966	8,309,966				
Administration expenses	5,962,080		5,698,133	5,698,133				
Finance costs	1,274,458		1,533,726	1,592,231				
Net (income) from operation	(164,589,045)		(164,593,724)	(164,535,219)		0.00%	-0.03%	0.04%
Income tax	20,612,645		20,574,216	20,625,416				
Net (Income)/Loss	(143,976,400)		(144,019,508)	(143,909,803)		0.03%	-0.05%	0.08%

Note 1. VAT returns do not include any financial information other than sales
Note 2. SAT returns do not include balance sheet information

EXHIBIT C-3

Reconciliations between Tax Reports and Management Accounts

Lihua Electron - 2010
All amounts in RMB
Debit (credit)

BALANCE SHEET	Management Accounts	VAT Return	SAT Return	SAIC Return	Variance: Management accounts vs. VAT Return	Variance: Management accounts vs. SAT Return	Variance: Management accounts vs. SAIC Return	SAT vs. SAIC
Current Assets								
Cash and cash equivalents	384,036,167			384,036,167			0.00%	
Account Receivable	94,735,569			94,735,569				
Notes receivables	3,500,600			3,500,600				
Other Receivables	65,480			61,905,195				
Inventory	35,712,318			35,712,318				
Intercompany	61,869,715							
Total current assets	579,919,849	-	-	579,888,849				
Non-current assets								
Net of PPE	46,975,866			46,975,866				
Construction in progress	1,086,375			1,086,375				
Intangible Assets	7,323,195			7,323,195				
Total Assets	635,305,285	-	-	635,275,285			0.00%	
Current Liabilities								
Account payable	(6,348,072)			(6,348,072)				
Other payables	(3,475,282)			(11,296,457)				
Income tax payable	(16,301,814)							
Tax payables	(1,691,097)			(17,622,507)				
Amount due to shareholder	(7,616,105)							
Other tax payables	(48,746)			(48,746)				
Accrued expenses	(22,125)			(22,125)				
Short - term loans	(15,000,000)			(15,000,000)				
Total current liabilities	(50,503,251)	-	-	(50,337,907)				
Shareholders' Equity								
Common stock -par value	(73,414,648)			(73,414,648)				
Additional paid in capital	(832,391)			(832,391)				
Retained earnings	(473,847,674)			(473,983,018)				
PRC statutory reserve	(36,707,323)			(36,707,323)				
Total shareholder's equity	(584,802,034)	-	-	(584,937,378)				
Total equity and liabilities	(635,305,285)	-	-	(635,275,285)			0.00%	
	-	-	-	-				

INCOME STATEMENT	Management Account	VAT Return	SAT Return	SAIC Return	Variance: Management accounts vs. VAT Return	Variance: Management accounts vs. SAT Return	Variance: Management accounts vs. SAIC Return	SAT vs. SAIC
Revenue	(1,246,684,271)	(1,247,745,763)	(1,246,684,271)	(1,246,684,271)	0.09%	0.00%	0.00%	0.00%
Cost of Good Sold	996,986,148		996,986,148	996,986,148		0.00%	0.00%	0.00%
Sales tax and surcharges	552,896		552,896	552,896				
Gross Profit	(249,145,227)		(249,145,227)	(249,145,227)		0.00%	0.00%	0.00%
Other Income	(1,471,838)		(1,471,838)	(1,471,838)				
Selling expenses	10,219,593		10,219,593	10,218,593				
Administration expenses	6,664,234		6,383,930	6,383,930				
Finance costs	(412,118)		(230,883)	(230,883)				
Other Expenses	874,195		33,450	874,195				
Net (income) from operation	(233,271,161)		(234,210,975)	(233,370,230)		0.40%	0.04%	0.36%
Income tax	58,603,945		58,552,744	58,462,644				
Net (Income)/Loss	(174,667,216)		(175,658,231)	(174,907,586)		0.57%	0.14%	0.43%

Note 1: VAT returns do not include any financial information other than sales
Note 2: SAT returns do not include balance sheet information

EXHIBIT C-4

Reconciliations between Tax Reports and Management Accounts

Libua Copper - 2008
All amounts in RMB
Debit (credit)

BALANCE SHEET

	Management Accounts	VAT Return	SAT Return	SAIC Return 2008 As filed	SAIC Return 2009 Comparative	Variance: Management accounts vs. VAT Return	Variance: Management accounts vs. SAT Return	Variance: Management accounts vs. SAIC Return 2008 As filed	Variance: Management accounts vs. SAIC Return 2009 Comp.	SAT vs. SAIC
Current Assets										
Cash and cash equivalents	10,812,820			1,948,145	10,812,820			-81.98%	0.00%	
Account Receivable										
Other AR				59,974,642	939,046					
Prepayment to suppliers				28,475,967	7,299,460					
Inventory										
Total current assets	10,812,820	-	-	90,398,753	19,051,325					
Non-current assets										
Net of PPE										
Construction in progress	41,130,221			2,900,766	40,258,875					
Intangible Assets	50,501,270			15,188,494	51,048,248					
Deposit for fixed assets	7,366,960									
Long term deferred expenses	159,893			178,313	75,803					
Total Assets	109,971,164	-	-	108,666,326	110,434,051			-1.19%	0.42%	
Current Liabilities										
Account payable	(192,306)				(192,306)					
Notes payable				(1,200,000)						
Other payables				(2,594,296)	(5,369,715)					
Tax payables										
Intercompany	(5,369,715)									
Total current liabilities	(5,562,021)	-	-	(3,794,296)	(5,562,021)					
Shareholders' Equity										
Common stock -par value	(104,872,030)			(104,872,030)	(104,872,030)					
Additional paid in capital										
Retained earnings	462,885									
PRC statutory reserve										
Total shareholder's equity	(104,409,145)	-	-	(104,872,030)	(104,872,030)					
Total equity and liabilities	(109,971,164)	-	-	(108,666,326)	(110,434,051)			-1.19%	0.42%	
	-	-	-	-	-					

INCOME STATEMENT

	Management Accounts	VAT Return	SAT Return	SAIC Return 2008 As filed	SAIC Return 2009 Comparative	Variance: Management accounts vs. VAT Return	Variance: Management accounts vs. SAT Return	Variance: Management accounts vs. SAIC Return 2008 As filed	Variance: Management accounts vs. SAIC Return 2009 Comp.	SAT vs. SAIC
Revenue			-	-	-					
Cost of Good Sold			-	-	-					
Gross Profit	-		-	-	-					
Other Income										
Selling expenses			-	-	-					
Administration expenses	563,769		-	-	-		-100.00%	-100.00%	-100.00%	0.00%
Finance costs			-	-	-					
Other Expenses			-	-	-					
Net loss from operations	563,769		-	-	-		-100.00%	-100.00%	-100.00%	0.00%
Income tax	(159,893)		-	-	-		-100.00%	-100.00%	-100.00%	0.00%
Net loss	403,876		-	-	-		-100.00%	-100.00%	-100.00%	0.00%

Note 1: VAT returns do not include any financial information other than sales
Note 2: SAT returns do not include balance sheet information
Note 3: "2009 Comparative" column is taken from prior year (2008) comparative column on the 2009 SAIC report

EXHIBIT C-5

Reconciliations between Tax Reports and Management Accounts

Lihua Copper - 2009
All amounts in RMB
Debit (credit)

BALANCE SHEET

	Management Accounts	VAT Return	SAT Return	SAIC Return	Variance – Management accounts vs. VAT Return	Variance – Management accounts vs. SAT Return	Variance – Management accounts vs. SAIC Return	Variance – SAT vs. SAIC
Current Assets								
Cash and cash equivalents	25,497,079			25,497,079			0.00%	
Account Receivable	15,580,315			15,580,315				
Prepayment to suppliers	118,112			294,512				
Taxes paid	3,248,231							
Inventory	76,376,471			76,376,471				
Total current assets	120,820,208	-	-	117,748,377				
Non-current assets								
Net of PPE	71,126,883			70,690,641				
Construction in progress	406,674			406,674				
Intangible Assets	48,480,375			49,480,375				
Deposit for fixed assets	176,400							
Long term deferred expenses				1,970,621				
Total Assets	242,010,540	-	-	240,296,688			-0.71%	
Current Liabilities								
Account payable	(23,271,284)			(23,271,282)				
Other payables	(226,471)			(62,096,186)				
Income tax payable	(4,571,014)							
Tax payables				(1,902,969)				
Intercompany	(61,869,715)							
Total current liabilities	(89,938,484)	-	-	(87,270,437)				
Shareholders' Equity								
Common stock -par value	(104,872,030)			(104,939,526)				
Additional paid in capital				(9,222)				
Retained earnings	(42,487,604)			(43,269,753)				
PRC statutory reserve	(4,712,422)			(4,807,750)				
Total shareholder's equity	(152,072,056)	-	-	(153,026,251)				
Total equity and liabilities	(242,010,540)	-	-	(240,296,688)			-0.71%	

INCOME STATEMENT

	Management Account	VAT Return	SAT Return	SAIC Return	Variance – Management Accounts as compared to: VAT Return	SAT Return	SAIC Return	
Revenue	(746,843,412)	(750,264,609)	(746,843,412)	(746,843,412)	0.46%	0.00%	0.00%	0.00%
Cost of Good Sold	676,794,039		678,119,874	675,746,301		0.20%	-0.15%	0.35%
Gross Profit	(70,049,373)		(68,723,538)	(71,097,111)		-1.89%	1.50%	-3.45%
Other Income	(3,421,197)			(3,421,197)				
Selling expenses	3,454,671			3,454,671				
Administration expenses	6,620,381			6,118,785				
Finance costs	(171,060)			(156,107)				
Other Expenses			5,748,454					
Net (income) from operation	(63,566,578)		(62,975,084)	(65,100,959)		-0.93%	2.41%	-3.38%
Income tax	15,903,664		15,743,771	16,483,850		-1.01%	3.65%	-4.70%
Net (Income)/Loss	(47,662,914)		(47,231,313)	(48,617,109)		-0.91%	2.00%	-2.93%

Note 1: VAT returns do not include any financial information other than sales
Note 2: SAT returns do not include balance sheet information

EXHIBIT C-6
Reconciliations between Tax Reports and Management Accounts

Lihua Copper - 2010
All amounts in RMB
Debit (credit)

BALANCE SHEET

	Management Accounts	VAT Return	SAT Return	SAIC Return	Variance: Management accounts vs. VAT Return	Variance: Management accounts vs. SAT Return	Variance: Management accounts vs. SAIC Return	Variance: SAT vs. SAIC
Current Assets								
Cash and cash equivalents	211,130,821			211,130,821			0.00%	
Account Receivable	123,639,377			123,639,377				
Other Receivables	80,000			80,000				
Prepayment to suppliers	-			132,550				
Inventory	73,253,056			73,253,056				
Total current assets	408,103,254	-	-	408,235,804				
Non-current assets								
Net of PPE	73,486,113			70,637,646				
Construction in progress	4,985,200			5,330,200				
Intangible Assets	116,930,509			116,930,509				
Deferred income tax assets	350,700							
Long term deferred expenses				3,353,113				
Total Assets	603,855,776	-	-	604,487,272			0.10%	
Current Liabilities								
Account payable	(33,467,834)			(35,866,834)				
Other payables	(2,816,331)			(62,388,945)				
Income tax payable	(16,688,390)			-				
Tax payables	(10,075,432)			(26,214,359)				
Amount due to shareholder	(61,869,715)			-				
Other tax payables	(360,564)			-				
Total current liabilities	(125,378,266)	-	-	(124,468,238)				
Shareholders' Equity								
Common stock -par value	(316,557,926)			(316,557,926)				
Additional paid in capital	(9,222)			(9,222)				
Retained earnings	(145,726,906)			(147,106,697)				
PRC statutory reserve	(16,183,456)			(16,345,189)				
Total shareholder's equity	(478,477,510)	-	-	(480,019,034)				
Total equity and liabilities	(603,855,776)	-	-	(604,487,272)			0.10%	
	^	^	^	^				

INCOME STATEMENT

	Management Account	VAT Return	SAT Return	SAIC Return	Variance: Management accounts vs. VAT Return	Variance: Management accounts vs. SAT Return	Variance: Management accounts vs. SAIC Return	Variance: SAT vs. SAIC
Revenue	(1,954,505,591)	(1,957,612,018)	(1,954,612,018)	(1,954,505,591)	0.16%	0.01%	0.00%	0.01%
Cost of Good Sold	1,783,967,899		1,784,652,632	1,784,652,632		0.04%	0.04%	0.00%
Sales tax and surcharges	983,847		983,847	983,846				
Gross Profit	(169,553,845)		(168,975,539)	(168,869,113)		-0.34%	-0.40%	0.06%
Other Income	(106,427)			(106,427)				
Selling expenses	3,714,225		3,714,225	3,714,225				
Administration expenses	12,089,503		11,348,338	11,348,338				
Finance costs	(477,580)		(554,297)	(554,297)				
Other Expenses	250,000		250,000	250,000				
Net (income) from operation	(154,084,124)		(154,219,273)	(154,219,274)		0.09%	0.09%	0.00%
Income tax	39,373,790		38,554,818	38,844,891				
Net (Income)/Loss	(114,710,334)		(115,664,455)	(115,374,383)		0.83%	0.58%	0.25%

Note 1: VAT returns do not include any financial information other than sales
Note 2: SAT returns do not include balance sheet information

Unless otherwise stated, Thornhill Capital relied upon the accuracy and completeness of information and data provided to us by the Company and its representatives. We have not independently verified the information or documentation provided to us unless expressly stated in this report. This report reflects all information provided to us by the Company, and obtained by us, up to the date of the final report. We have no responsibility to update this report for, nor do we make any representation about the impact of, events and circumstances occurring after the date of this report. There are other areas, such as issues of law, tax, regulatory issues, and other specialized areas where we do not have expertise, which are outside the scope of our review and may be relevant. You should consider whether to obtain expert advice in relation to these areas. All of the information presented herein is qualified by the accuracy and completeness of the information provided to us by the Company and its representatives.

No information included in this report is intended or should be construed as any advice, recommendation or endorsement from us as to any legal, tax, investment or other matter. You alone will need to evaluate the merits and risks associated with the use of this report as they relate to any underlying securities of the subject entity. Decisions based on information obtained from the report are your sole responsibility, and before making any investment decision, you should consider (with or without the assistance of a securities advisor) whether the information is appropriate in light of your particular investment needs, objectives and financial circumstances. Investors should seek financial advice regarding the suitability of investing in any securities.

No reference to any specific security constitutes a recommendation to buy, sell or hold that security or any other security. Nothing in this report shall be considered a solicitation or offer to buy or sell any security, future, option or other financial instrument or to offer or provide any investment advice or service to any person in any jurisdiction. Nothing contained on the website constitutes investment advice or offers any opinion with respect to the suitability of any security, and the views expressed in this report should not be taken as advice to buy, sell or hold any security. In preparing the information contained in this report, we have not taken into account the investment needs, objectives and/or financial circumstances of any particular investor.

The objective of our report is to provide comprehensive details on a variety of findings as described therein. Our report may include tests of the Company's accounting records and other procedures we consider appropriate to help us reach conclusions outlined in the report. The report includes examining, on a test basis, evidence supporting certain amounts and disclosure in the Company's financial statements; therefore, our report will involves judgment about the number of transactions to be examined and the areas to be tested. We have not performed such testing on all aspects of the Company's financial statements, and we have not performed an audit of the financial statements, and we therefore have not issued any opinion about whether the Company's financial statements as a whole are materially correct.

Any views expressed in this report were prepared based upon the information available to us at the time such views were written. Changed or additional information could cause such views to change. All information is subject to possible correction. Information may quickly become unreliable for various reasons, including changes in market conditions or economic circumstances.

APPENDIX B
Disclaimers

Whether you're in China, the US, or any other part of the world, no two due diligence assignments will ever be the same. The facts and circumstances will always vary based on innumerable factors, such as company size, industry, geography, competitive landscape, government regulations, geopolitical and macroeconomic forces, and social trends. All of these factors will affect how a due diligence assignment is planned and carried out.

It's impossible to create a *one size fits all* guide to performing due diligence on all companies. Rather, in writing this book, our goal is to provide a framework to explain the important differences between business practices that might be used in the West, and those employed in China. In accomplishing this we provide a reasonable methodology for independently analyzing those practices.

Many of the procedures detailed herein, such as cash and tax verification procedures, for example, are common to the vast majority of companies. Others, such as inventory analysis, channel checks, and fixed asset verification are specific to more *traditional* manufacturing or distribution entities. The procedures outlined in *Piercing the Great Wall of Corporate China* will not apply to each and every assignment, and careful consideration must be given to the dynamics of any situation before applying any of the procedures that we describe. Furthermore, there are certain areas that we touch upon in this book including, but not limited to, legal and intellectual property matters, which may require the assistance of highly specialized experts outside of a standard due diligence team.

Any claims, assertions and advice regarding Chinese business and due diligence practices are based on our research, and on our experience in dealing with many Chinese companies, executives, advisors, and government officials in a variety of industries and situations.

The information, ideas, and suggestions in *Piercing the Great Wall of Corporate China* are not intended as a substitute for professional legal or accounting advice. Before following any suggestions contained in this book, consult your attorney or accounting professional, as appropriate. Neither the author nor the publisher shall be liable or responsible for any loss or damage allegedly arising as a consequence of your use or application of any information or suggestions in *Piercing the Great Wall of Corporate China*.

There's no guaranteed path to a successful due diligence engagement in China. However, we believe that understanding the nuances of doing business there, and applying the principles we've outlined, will give you a much better opportunity for avoiding the common pitfalls that we've witnessed in many due diligence reports on Chinese companies.

Endnotes

1 "Foreign Audit Firms and US-Listed Chinese Companies," Shanghai Expat, http://www.shanghaiexpat.com/phpbbforum/foreign-audit-firms-us-listed-chinese-companies-t149652.html.

2 Jack Welch, "China Quotes," Brainy Quote, http://www.brainyquote.com/quotes/keywords/china.html.

3 "Due Diligence," Merriam-Webster, http://www.merriam-webster.com/dictionary/due%20diligence.

4 "Forensic Due Diligence—Don't Invest Without It," Forensico, http://www.forensicopartners.com/userfiles/Forensic%20Due%20Diligence%20-Dont%20Invest%20Without%20It(4).pdf.

5 "Financial Due Diligence and Transaction Support," BDO Consulting, http://bdoconsulting.com/services/due-diligence-financial.aspx.

6 Noah Waisberg, "Legal Due Diligence Explained," DiligenceEngine, http://blog.diligenceengine.com/2011/06/09/legal-due-diligence-explained/.

7 Arthur H. Rosenbloom, *Due Diligence for Global Deal Making* (New York: Bloomberg Press, 2002), 7–9.

8 "Due Diligence Checklist Operations," Merger Integration, http://merger-integration.com.au/due-diligence-checklist-operations/.

9 "Articles of Association," *Investopedia*, http://www.investopedia.com/terms/a/articles-of-association.asp#axzz24TBdRVJD.

10 Myron Tay, "China—Incorporation Capabilities—A Certification and Notarization Perspective," *Scribd*, http://www.scribd.com/doc/12507114/China-Incorporation-Capacities-A-Certification-Notarization-Perspective.

11 "Performing Legal Due Diligence in China," Inveiss, http://www.inveiss.com/main/performing-legal-due-diligence-in-china.

12 "Starting a Business in China," World Bank Group, http://www.doingbusiness.org/data/exploreeconomies/china/starting-a-business/.

13 "About 'People's Republic of China Organization Code Certificate,'" Trade, http://www.trade.cn/article/reference/51.html.

14 Jason Tian, "The Legal Implication of Corporate Seal in Chinese Corporate Practice," Chinese Lawyer in Shanghai, http://www.sinoblawg.com/?p=341.

15 "Organization Code Certificate," *Practical Law*, http://www.uk.practicallaw.com/5-530-5687?source=relatedcontent.

16 "Understanding China's 'Fapiao' Invoice System," China Briefing, http://www.china-briefing.com/news/2013/08/13/understanding-chinas-fapiao-invoice-system.html.

17 Terence Wong. "Acquisition of a Business Due Diligence Checklist," Forbo Siegling China, http://www.slideshare.net/wongkm/due-diligence-checklist-11568348.

18 "A Brief History of Intellectual Property in China and India," *techdirt*, http://www.techdirt.com/articles/20090530/1620345062.shtml.

19 Randall R. Rader, "Intellectual Property Protection in China," *The Federalist Society for Law and Public Policy Studies*, http://www.fed-soc.org/publications/detail/intellectual-property-protection-in-china.

20 "PCAOB Oversees the Auditors of Companies to Protect Investors," Public Company Accounting Oversight Board, http://pcaobus.org/Pages/default.aspx.

21 "Listing in the US: A Guide to a Listing of Equity Securities on NASDAQ and NYSE," PricewaterhouseCoopers, http://www.pwc.com/en_UA/ua/services/capital-markets/assets/listing-in-the-us-ua-en.pdf.

22 Matthew Moss, Brian Ross, and Stuart Johnson, "US Officials: China Refuses to Help Stop Investment Scams," ABC News, http://abcnews.go.com/Blotter/us-investors-lose-billions-alleged-chinese-stock-schemes/story?id=18164787&singlePage=true.

23 Dr. Vivian Lee, "Understanding the Organizational Structure of Chinese Companies," Dragon Business Network, http://www.dragonbn.com/articles/140.

24 "Chinese Management Style," WorldBusinessCulture, http://www.worldbusinessculture.com/Chinese-Management-Style.html.

25 Doug Guthrie and Junmin Wang, *Handbook of Research on Asian Business* (Northampton: Edward Elgar Publishing Inc., 2006), 99-116.

26 Kai Chang and William Brown, "From Individual to Collective Labor Relations: Transformation of Collective Labor Relations and Evolution of Labor Policy in China," School of Labor and Human Resources, Renmin University of China, July 2002, http://ilera2012.wharton.upenn.edu/NonRefereedPapers/Kai,%20Chang%20and%20Brown,%20William.pdf.

27 "Labor and Social Security in China," Information Office of the State Council of the People's Republic of China, April 2002, http://news.xinhuanet.com/zhengfu/2002-11/18/content_633162.htm.

28 Adam Livermore. "Clarifying 2010 Employment Contracts," *China Briefing*, January 11, 2010, http://www.china-briefing.com/news/2010/01/11/clarifying-2010-employment-contracts.html.

29 Xia Chao and Michael Droke, "Employee vs. Independent Contractor," *Shanghai Business Review*, November 2010, http://www.dorsey.com/files/upload/Employee_VS_Independent_110910.pdf.

30 Arnold Ji, "Compensation and Benefit Policy in China," MS Motor Service Asia Pacific Co., Ltd., March 29, 2012, http://www.nordiccentre.org/downloads/MA_2012/china_wage_policy.pdf.

31 "Equity-Based Compensation Plan," PricewaterhouseCoopers, http://www.pwccn.com/home/eng/ias_cnhk_compensation_plan.html.

32 Shirley Brown and Irene Yu, "Equity Based Compensation in China," Deloitte, February 29, 2008, http://www.amcham-shanghai.org/amchamportal/InfoVault_Library/2008/Equity_Based_Compensation_in_China.pdf.

33 Calista Huang and Zhengyi Zhang, "China Securities Regulatory Commission Intends to Launch the 'Employee Stock Ownership Plans of Listed Companies,'" *LLinks Corporate Finance Bulletin,* September 2012, LLinks Law Offices, http://www.llinkslaw.com/shangchuan/20130105122231.pdf.

34 Yuping Wang and Kevin Moore, "Producing an Effective Employment Handbook in China," Davis Wright Tremaine LLP, April 13, 2009, http://www.dwt.com/advisories/ Producing_an_Effective_Employment_Handbook_in_China_04_13_2009/.

35 "Off-Balance-Sheet Financing," *Investopedia*, http://www.investopedia.com/terms/o/obsf.asp.

36 "Taxation in China," China-Window.com, http://www.china-window.com/china_market/investment_in_china/taxation-in-china.shtml.

37 Joyce Yanyun Man, "China's Property Tax Reform: Progress and Challenges," *Land Lines*, April 2012, Lincoln Institute of Land Policy, http://www.lincolninst.edu/pubs/PubDetail.aspx?pubid=2022&URL=China-s-Property-Tax-Reform&Page=4.

38 Mary Swire. "China Changes Vehicle Taxes from January 1," *Tax-News,* December 23, 2011, http://www.tax-news.com/news/china_changes_vehicle_taxes_from_january_1____53090.html.

39 "China Kicks Off National Resource Tax Reform," *China Briefing*, October 13, 2011, http://www.china-briefing.com/news/2011/10/13/china-kicks-off-national-resource-tax-reform.html.

40 "China's Current Tax System—Vehicle and Vessel Usage Tax," *Kaizen Corporate Services* Limited, http://www.by-cpa.com/html/news/20076/596.html.

41 "Vessel Tonnage Tax Taxpayers and Tax Base," China Business Engine, http://www.cbize.com/upload/document/atta%20vessel%20tonnage%20taxpayers.pdf.

42 "Guide to China Workplace Laws and Regulations," *Kingfisher PLC,* http://files.the-group.net/library/kgf/responsibility/pdfs/cr_13.pdf.

43 Ronald C. Brown, *Understanding Labor and Employment Law in China* (Cambridge: Cambridge University Press, 2010), 37.

44 Ronald C. Brown, *East Asian Labor and Employment Law* (Cambridge: Cambridge University Press, 2012), 420.

45 Brown, *Understanding Labor and Employment*, 38–39.

46 "Patent and Trademark Protection in China," China IPR SME Helpdesk, http://www.slideshare.net/IPRChina/8-china-ipr-helpdesk-patent-and-trademark-protection-in-china.

47 "Copyright Protection in China: Know Before You Go," China IPR SME Helpdesk, http://www.china-iprhelpdesk.eu/sites/all/docs/publications/EN_Copyright_guide_Aug_2010.pdf.

48 Stephen M. Perl, *Doing Business with China: The Secrets of Dancing with the Dragon* (Lexington: ChinaMart USA Book Publishing Inc., 2012), 45.

49 "Overview of China's Current Tax System," AsiaTradeHub.com, http://www.asiatradehub.com/china/tax.asp.

50 "China's Tax System," State Administration of Taxation of the People's Republic of China, http://www.chinatax.gov.cn/2013/n2925/.

51 Rita Bolt Barker and Mauri Lawrence, "Sample Buyer's Environmental Due Diligence Checklist," Wyche, https://www.wyche.com/articles/sample-buyers-environmental-due-diligence-checklist/.

52 Zhouman Liao and Lijie Zhu, "Regaining Investor Confidence for US-Listed Chinese Companies," *The Financial Professionals' Post*, January 17, 2012, New York Society of Security Analysts, http://post.nyssa.org/nyssa-news/2012/01/regaining-investor-confidence-for-us-listed-chinese-companies.html.

Index

F

G

H

I

J

L

M

N

O

P

Q

R

S

T

U

V

W

Z

Bibliography

AsiaTradeHub.com. "Overview of China's Current Tax System." http://www.asiatradehub.com/china/tax.asp.

BDO Consulting. "Financial Due Diligence and Transaction Support." http://bdoconsulting.com/services/due-diligence-financial.aspx.

Bolt Barker, Rita, and Maurie Lawrence. "Sample Buyer's Environmental Due Diligence Checklist." Wyche. http://www.wyche.com/article/sample-buyer%E2%80%99s-environmental-due-diligence-checklist.

Brown, Ronald C. *East Asian Labor and Employment Law.* Cambridge: Cambridge University Press, 2012.

———. *Understanding Labor and Employment Law in China.* Cambridge: Cambridge University Press, 2010.

Brown, Shirley, and Irene Yu. "Equity Based Compensation in China." Deloitte. February 29, 2008. http://www.amcham-shanghai.org/amchamportal/InfoVault_Library/2008/Equity_Based_Compensation_in_China.pdf.

Carder, Kirby. "The National Organization Code is a Necessary Step in the Post CIRC Approval Process to Open a Chinese Representative Office." *China Insurance Law.* http://www.china-insurance-law.com/chinese-insurance-market-information/the-national-organization-code-certificate-is-a-necessary-step-in-the-post-circ-approval-process-to-open-a-chinese-representative-office/.

Chang, Kai, and William Brown. "From Individual to Collective Labor Relations: Transformation of Collective Labor Relations and

Evolution of Labor Policy in China." School of Labor and Human Resources, Renmin University of China. July 2002. http://ilera2012.wharton.upenn.edu/NonRefereedPapers/Kai,%20Chang%20and%20Brown,%20William.pdf.

Chao, Xia, and Michael Droke. "Employee vs. Independent Contractor." *Shanghai Business Review.* November 2010. http://www.dorsey.com/files/upload/Employee_VS_Independent_110910.pdf.

China Briefing. "China Kicks Off National Resource Tax Reform." October 13, 2011. http://www.china-briefing.com/news/2011/10/13/china-kicks-off-national-resource-tax-reform.html.

———. "Understanding China's 'Fapiao' Invoice System." http://www.china-briefing.com/news/2013/08/13/understanding-chinas-fapiao-invoice-system.html.

China Business Engine. "Vessel Tonnage Tax Taxpayers and Tax Base." http://www.cbize.com/upload/document/atta%20vessel%20tonnage%20taxpayers.pdf.

China IPR SME Helpdesk. "Copyright Protection in China: Know Before You Go." http://www.own-it.org/uploads/files/330/original/Copyright_Protection_in_China.pdf.

———. "Patent and Trademark Protection in China." http://www.slideshare.net/IPRChina/8-china-ipr-helpdesk-patent-and-trademark-protection-in-china.

China-Window.com. "Taxation in China." http://www.china-window.com/china market/investment in china/taxation-in-china.shtml.

Forensico. "Forensic Due Diligence—Don't Invest Without It." http://www.forensicopartners.com/userfiles/Forensic%20Due%20Diligence%20-Dont%20Invest%20Without%20It(4).pdf.

Guthrie, Doug, and Junmin Wang. *Handbook of Research on Asian Business.* Northampton: Edward Elgar Publishing Inc., 2006.

Huang, Calista, and Zhengyi Zhang. "China Securities Regulatory Commission Intends to Launch the 'Employee Stock Ownership Plans of Listed Companies.'" *LLinks Corporate Finance Bulletin.*

September 2012. LLinks Law Offices. http://www.llinkslaw.com/shangchuan/20130105122231.pdf.

Information Office of the State Council of the People's Republic of China. "Labor and Social Security in China." April 2002. http://news.xinhuanet.com/zhengfu/2002-11/18/content_633162.htm.

Inveiss. "Performing Legal Due Diligence in China." http://www.inveiss.com/performing-legal-due-diligence-in-china.

Investopedia. "Articles of Association." http://www.investopedia.com/terms/a/articles-of-association.asp#axzz24TBdRVJD.

———. "Off-Balance-Sheet Financing." http://www.investopedia.com/terms/o/obsf.asp.

Ji, Arnold. "Compensation and Benefit Policy in China," MS Motor Service Asia Pacific Co., Ltd. March 29, 2012. http://www.nordiccentre.org/downloads/MA_2012/china_wage_policy.pdf.

Kaizen Corporate Services Limited. "China's Current Tax System—Vehicle and Vessel Usage Tax." http://www.by-cpa.com/html/news/20076/596.html.

Kingfisher PLC. "Guide to China Workplace Laws and Regulations." http://files.the-group.net/library/kgf/responsibility/pdfs/cr_13.pdf.

Lee, Dr. Vivian. "Understanding the Organizational Structure of Chinese Companies." Dragon Business Network. http://www.dragonbn.com/articles/140.

Liao, Zhouman, and Lijie Zhu. "Regaining Investor Confidence for US-Listed Chinese Companies." *The Financial Professionals' Post* (January 17, 2012). New York Society of Security Analysts, http://post.nyssa.org/nyssa-news/2012/01/regaining-investor-confidence-for-us-listed-chinese-companies.html.

Livermore, Adam. "Clarifying 2010 Employment Contracts." *China Briefing*. January 11, 2010. http://www.china-briefing.com/news/2010/01/11/clarifying-2010-employment-contracts.html.

Man, Joyce Yanyun. "China's Property Tax Reform: Progress and Challenges." *Land Lines* (April 2012). Lincoln

Institute of Land Policy. http://www.lincolninst.edu/pubs/PubDetail.aspx?pubid=2022&URL=China-s-Property-Tax-Reform&Page=4.

Merger Integration. "Due Diligence Checklist Operations." http://merger-integration.com.au/due-diligence-checklist-operations/.

Merriam-Webster. "Due Diligence." http://www.merriam-webster.com/dictionary/due%20diligence.

Mosk, Matthew, Brian Ross, and Stuart Johnson. "US Officials: China Refuses to Help Stop Investment Scams." ABC News. http://abcnews.go.com/Blotter/us-investors-lose-billions-alleged-chinese-stock-schemes/story?id=18164787&singlePage=true.

Perl, Stephen M. *Doing Business with China: The Secrets of Dancing with the Dragon*. Lexington: ChinaMart USA Book Publishing Inc., 2012.

PricewaterhouseCoopers. "Equity-Based Compensation Plan." http://www.pwccn.com/home/eng/ias_cnhk_compensation_plan.html.

________. "Listing in the US: A Guide to a Listing of Equity Securities on NASDAQ and NYSE." http://www.pwc.com/en_UA/ua/services/capital-markets/assets/listing-in-the-us-ua-en.pdf.

Public Company Accounting Oversight Board. "PCAOB Oversees the Auditors of Companies to Protect Investors." http://pcaobus.org/Pages/default.aspx.

Rader, Randall R. "Intellectual Property Protection in China." *The Federalist Society for Law and Public Policy Studies.* http://www.fed-soc.org/publications/detail/intellectual-property-protection-in-china.

Rosenbloom, Arthur H. *Due Diligence for Global Deal Making*. New York: Bloomberg Press, 2002.

Shanghai Expat. "Foreign Audit Firms & US-Listed Chinese Companies." http://www.shanghaiexpat.com/phpbbforum/foreign-audit-firms-us-listed-chinese-companies-t149652.html.

State Administration of Taxation of the People's Republic of China. "China's Tax System." http://www.chinatax.gov.cn/n6669073/n6669133/6887407.html.

Swire, Mary. "China Changes Vehicle Taxes from January 1." *Tax-News*. December 23, 2011. http://www.tax-news.com/news/china_changes_vehicle_taxes_from_january_1____53090.html.

Tay, Myron. "China—Incorporation Capabilities—A Certification and Notarization Perspective." *Scribd*. http://www.scribd.com/doc/12507114/China-Incorporation-Capacities-A-Certification-Notarization-Perspective.

Techdirt. "A Brief History of Intellectual Property in China and India." http://www.techdirt.com/articles/20090530/1620345062.shtml.

Tian, Jason. "The Legal Implication of Corporate Seal in Chinese Corporate Practice." Chinese Lawyer in Shanghai. http://www.sinoblawg.com/?p=341.

Trade.cn. "About 'People's Republic of China Organization Code Certificate.'" http://www.trade.cn/article/reference/51.html.

Waisberg, Noah. "Legal Due Diligence Explained." DiligenceEngine. http://blog.diligenceengine.com/2011/06/09/legal-due-diligence-explained/.

Wang, Yuping, and Kevin Moore. "Producing an Effective Employment Handbook in China," Davis Wright Tremaine LLP. April 13, 2009. http://www.dwt.com/advisories/Producing_an_Effective_Employment_Handbook_in_China_04_13_2009/.

Welch, Jack. "China Quotes." Brainy Quote. http://www.brainyquote.com/quotes/keywords/china.html.

Wong, Terence. "Acquisition of a Business Due Diligence Checklist." Forbo Siegling China. http://www.slideshare.net/wongkm/due-diligence-checklist-11568348.

World Bank Group. "Starting a Business in China." http://www.doingbusiness.org/data/exploreeconomies/china/starting-a-business/.

WorldBusinessCulture. "Chinese Management Style." http://www.worldbusinessculture.com/Chinese-Management-Style.html.

About the Authors

Alan Refkin is the Chairman and CEO of Thornhill Capital, a global consulting firm. He is an internationally recognized expert on China and has worked there on numerous projects for more than a decade. He's spoken on financial, management, and joint venture topics at the National People's Congress in Beijing and at numerous Chinese government seminars. Mr. Refkin has published three critically acclaimed books on how to conduct business in China and writes a column on Chinese business practices for an international newspaper.

Mr. Refkin has also lectured internationally on how to perform due diligence on Chinese companies, protecting one's intellectual property in China, and negotiating with the Chinese government and its business community. He currently serves as an adviser to a number of US, Chinese, and international corporations and financial institutions. More information on the author, including his blogs and newsletters, can be obtained at www.alanrefkin.com and www.thrornhillcapital.net.

David A. Dodge has been an independent financial consultant since 2007, providing a wide variety of financial and accounting services to public and private companies around the globe. He has acted as a CFO and/or provided financial accounting, reporting, and compliance services for multiple public and private companies in the US, Canada, England, and China as well as privately held Chinese companies seeking to raise capital in North America. He has also supervised and authored dozens of forensic due diligence reviews on Chinese companies in a variety of industries. Moreover, Mr. Dodge has acted as an accounting expert witness and expert consultant in China-based and other shareholder litigation.

Mr. Dodge was an auditor with Ernst & Young LLP from 1997 to 1999 and holds a BA in economics from Yale University and an MS in accounting from the University of Hartford.

Printed in the United States
By Bookmasters